SHINE YOUR
DIVINE
LIGHT

Tapping into your inner power
to transform your life

SHINE YOUR DIVINE LIGHT

Tapping into your inner power to transform your life

Written by Neferatiti Ife

Shine your Divine light
Written by Neferatiti Ife

2nd print published July 2016
By Sun Ra Publishing Ltd, UK

SUN RA
PUBLISHING

www.neferatitiife.com
neferatiti@googlemail.com

Designer: Kwame Edwards of Rising Generations CIC
Cover illustration Artist: Alvin Kofi of KOFI ARTS
Neffy cartoons: Onyiye Iwu
Proof reading: Sam Amalemba and Danni Blencher

Contents

I give Thanks to Almighty Creator - Mother/Father God,

My Ancestors, The spirit world, My Partner, My family
and the future generations who may read this book
and gain clarity and insight in their lives.

Preface

We are all looking for love, happiness and a contented life however, all too often, these feelings of love and contentment can be moments in our lives that never remain constant long enough to fully appreciate. There is a way to a more lasting happiness and permanent feelings of contentment that can transform your mind, body and spirit. To reach this place the individual has to go on a journey into Self in order to heal Self and to discover the golden nugget that is you. Beyond your ego, beyond your personality, beyond the physical, beyond your emotional space arriving at a place of Divine essence. This book will take you on this journey to find healing, contentment and self-activation.

In the Western world we are told that contentment and happiness are found in the material things we buy or consume. We are constantly being sold the idea that we are somehow lacking and therefore need external resources and material gain in order to make us feel better. We might even take a holiday to take us away to a little sunshine and happiness but it's all just a temporary fix. All too often these are moments in our lives that never stay long enough, leaving us back where we started fighting off emotional unhappiness, depression and the drudgery of work or unemployment. We don't feel happiness within ourselves and often we find all kinds of distractions and addictions to soothe the inner turmoil. Even those who live the most luxurious lives are often just as depressed, as they realise money can't buy happiness, love and contentment. Of course everyone should live a life of abundance, this is our Divine gift, but not one rooted in selfishness, conquest and greed.

This only brings emotional emptiness. The truth is most of us, regardless of status, just can't find the things we need most and the more we chase the more it runs away. We may have many Facebook friends, but we are still lonely, we are looking for love but we are still single, we want to move forward in life but we're stuck in the mud of life.

This book opens the door and lets the sunshine and fresh air into your life. It is based on the premise that you are the master of your destiny, able to heal self, break the psychological patterns and create happiness and abundance in your life. Life will no longer be a struggle because you are now working with the laws of attraction.

So many of us are trapped or weighed down by our past, childhood experiences, family, ancestral lineage, lovers, partners etc. Only a few of us know how to find a way out of this entanglement. So we just wear a mask to hide ourselves, from the world and pretend that it doesn't affect us or we bury our heads in the sand whilst deep inside we are feeling the emotional baggage expressed in our unhappiness. We are all guilty of wearing the mask; it's a way to protect ourselves in a world that doesn't value vulnerability or honesty so we learn to hide our feelings. We learn to be like the crowd whilst at the same time, the real you is dying. The real authentic you cannot express itself in the fog of denial. All your pent up feelings get pushed further and further away in the closet of your hearts and bloodstream. What we are not taught is that there is a price to be paid for wearing the mask, for being in denial. That price is unhappiness, that price is addiction, that price is cancer and all manner of illnesses.

You are reading this book because deep down you realise it's
 time for change. Time to move on, to get what you truly deserve.
Now is the opportunity to transform your life and find the answers
to the questions we rarely ask ourselves. How do I heal from a
broken heart? How do I heal from the trauma of the past? How do
I move away from addictions (drink, drugs, games, work) that is
destroying my body and taking me off the road to contentment??
Like most of us, Neferatiti Ife has been on the same journey asking
the same questions. She took her questions to the highest of the
highest Mother/Father Creator and her Kemetian (Egyptian)
ancestors. Through this connection and her great ability to channel
this wisdom, she has come forth with this deeply profound book.
In doing so she has opened a door to a unique universe that is able
to transform our lives individually and bring forth profound truths
about our existence.

Menelik Shabazz

Introduction
WHY AND WHEREFORES

This book is a rare in the world of spirituality because it comes from a African/Caribbean/British perspective. My unusual twist is that I am a psychic channeller and I live in two worlds; both the physical and the spiritual .You will be reading about these two worlds and how they mesh together to assist and transform my life. I am truly blessed to have this wonderful, spiritual gift, which has been guiding me for the last twenty years. This guidance from the two dimensions has now created a synergy that has become my special, unique, self-empowerment journey. We all want to be happy and contented. We all want to meet our soul mate, have fulfilling relationships and be in constant love. We all want to be, at peace, devoid of all of those worrying thoughts. We all want positive self-esteem, to look young, beautiful and clever. We all want money, to be sexy and have a wonderful figure. We want the big house, big car, two point five children, great health, great sex and beautiful skin. Funnily enough. What is most important to us is that,

WE ALL WANT EVERYTHING NOW!
We all want TRANSFORMATION from the hell
that we are going through....

Amazingly, but what we need to consider. Our wishing for the above may not be the solution to our happiness. We need to look at what we desire and to realise in order to manifest them, we will have to change our mind set and internal vibration. This book can help you get some of the above because during the process of reading, you will be taken on a transformational journey. This book is steeped in an energy of powerful, deep internal self–inquiry. Promoting an ambiance of external and internal healing. Creating abundance and transformation of the mind, body and spirit.

You are reading this book because you want that inner peace and harmony. You want abundance and you want to be contented. Slaying your demons with one swipe. There is no ready-made pill, or else I would buy it! (joke) but by reading this book and following the exercises: Meditation, inner peace, harmony and transformation can be achieved. There is a deep need for healing in the African/ Caribbean community and the wider communities, worldwide.

There is general daily unhappiness in individuals' vibration leading to a crying out for some uplifting of each individual and community spirit. My feelings and thoughts come from years and years of going to meetings and listening to African and Caribbean's talk incessantly about our issues without any solution. I became frustrated with this talk shop of what we need to do. As people are good at offering advice but what about practical ideas of how to deal with everyday issues that affect each of us? Each and every month another Black young man dies in London and this situation has gone on for years and continues to go on without any in-depth looking at the deeper issues that concern the wider community. This book is written at a time when numbers of single people are increasing, divorce is increasing, and our children are struggling in society. Families are in decline, and the mental health institutions are filled with African/Caribbean men. These are the main fundamental issues that are affecting the community and individuals, and now is the time for change. This book looks at the human being at a very basic but deep level. It is to be used as a work book to address fundamental healing that can be used on an individual level however, this individual healing can then go on to create a collective consciousness movement. This much needed healing will allow you to realign yourself back to your true state, a peaceful harmonious self. Realigning back to this state, enables and equips each person with the tools to follow their life path and connect with their Divine Self. It is a workbook designed to empower through; my personal reflections, advice from the spirit world and exercises designed to question and explore your beliefs, truthfully honestly and wisely. The book incorporates the holistic self, the mind, the body, the spirit, the soul and the external world. The process I use for contacting the spirit world is via channelling. This is an experience of sitting, meditating and calling upon the spirit world for assistance. The words are not created from my mind but they are words that mentally come to me externally whilst in a trance state. For example a songwriter or musician is inspired to write a song but they are unaware where the inspiration came from. An Artist inspired to paint is also unaware of where the information comes from. Thus there is an unseen world of inspiration that we all can access when we are in a particular state of mind. This book contains words from the unseen world, words of guidance and power. Please note that the words from the spirit world are identified in a different font. They speak in with an unusual rhythm but take your time, and as you read their words the power will flow through. The information I receive connects us with the past; it influences the present, the future and provides solutions to some of our present issues. In the Chapters I use my own experiences as a template and I have received guidance from the spirit world for healing solutions. I write extensively about my self-esteem and "not feeling adequate enough". These feelings are universal for some and they present themselves in different areas in my life. These I share with you. For some of us the same issues reoccur in different arenas stopping and blocking us from abundance. You will notice that these issues are repeated in some of the chapters. The repetition is due to the same issue reoccurring in a different guise.

Each chapter ends with an exercise to assist the reader to delve into their own issues. We begin with looking at our families that we are born into, their story and how it affects us individually. This allows us to examine how we have emotionally processed the effects of family life.

In Chapter three, you will learn how meditation can assist your healing via breathing and calming your mind and body down. We will then go on to explore the effect of sound on the individual that is hugely significant on your well-being. If this sound comes to you in the form of words, you can be negatively/positively be affected by what has been said to you in the past and those unresolved feelings can manifest in present day life. Chapter five, considers music and its ability to change an individual's mood through the vibration of sound. In this chapter, you will have access to understanding the key effects of negative and positive sounds on our everyday thoughts and vibration. Every sound has a vibration that our bodies and energies soak up.

Subjects such as the ego is also explored as well as stress, money and their negative impact of the wider world. In each of these chapters, I consider my experience and the solutions that have assisted me. From the beginning to the middle of the book, the concentration is mainly about the obstacles that hinder us from becoming our Divine Self. The last chapters deal with the Self, intimate relationships, gratitude and forgiveness. The ending of the book looks for ways of transformation and healing from the inner world. This book will take you on a journey to examine the obstacles that hinder you from becoming your True, Divine Self. To this new self will be able to understand and exercise the healing power of forgiveness and gratitude in all relationships.

Understanding and exercising the power of forgiveness and gratitude. Whilst on this transformational journey you will encounter healing of your inner and outer worlds.

The Self is crying out for love and when we become equipped with this love, we can go on to love others. Reading this book provides an internal, individual in-depth look at how we all can resolve our inner issues and live a life of joy and contentment. When we, as individuals, come to awaken our own consciousness we can then open our arms to each other and create a community of higher vibration and healing.

We need love especially, self-love on an individual level and community level. The whole community needs love and healing. Now is time for the healing, self-success, transformation and abundance to start.

Meditation

Lets begin by getting ourselves into alignment with the information we are about to read.

Breathe in and then out. Keep breathing in and out and take large breaths allowing air to come in through your nose. Fill up your lungs and breathe in through your nose and then out through your mouth. Keep breathing in and out until you start to feel relaxed. This short breathing meditation is to open your spirit to Divine guidance. Carry on breathing in and then out ten times. Whilst breathing, let all of the worries and the cares fade away. This is a time to for you to connect within and to listen to the inner voice of the Divine connection our Creator Mother/ Father Principle.

Chapter 1
LEARNING FROM MY PERSONAL AWAKENING

Amazingly, but as usual, my spiritual awakening began with anger and frustration. There was a period in my life where I became angry with others and myself. Everything and anything was a problem and an argument. You would imagine that leaving the environment of a stressful, career in social work and working a 9-5 day. Would leave me feeling great but it didn't; it came with great difficulty. Although it was what I wanted to do, I made the mistake of thinking it would be easy. I didn't foresee any of the pitfalls, especially financially. Being spiritual and psychic was a path I chose to follow. This path has benefited me both in my personal and working life. My aim was, and is, to do what I know best: to empower others and to allow all to be who they were brought into this world to be. I had always been intuitive, had dreams and sometimes premonitions. I have always been drawn to the unknown world but felt uneasy speaking to others about my calling. The uneasiness meant that I hid my dreams and premonitions, fearing that I would be judged and not believed.

My spiritual/psychic journey really began seven years ago. At this point I began to take the spirit world seriously. I began to visit spiritual churches, attend personal development groups and listen to lectures on the subject of spirituality. Whist listening, I felt like an outsider even though I have been channelling, talking to spirits for seven years and had already co-written a psychic/spiritual book. I still felt inadequate and lacked confidence. It appeared that during this time, what was occurring was that I was actually putting others on a pedestal, unconsciously. Thinking that they were fantastic because they were able to connect with spirit, live and in front of other people. They seemed to be able to conduct spirit/psychic readings and to do all the things I was aiming to do easily and without effort.

They were able to give personal information and correct accurate readings to complete strangers. I found this quite amazing but also frustrating because what was beginning to unravel, were feelings of unworthiness in me. The stirring up of all of these negative thoughts and feelings brought on an emotional volcano and on the 07 of January 2012. The realisation, that shaped my path, and the sharp bitter truth was that, inside of me I felt, unable to attain what others were able to achieve. That I was actually saying to myself (and ultimately the wider world) was that I was not as good as these people. I genuinely believed that I could never be as good as them and with these feelings, I lost all of my confidence.

Once this inner revelation was declared painfully but honestly, other things began to open up. This day was special because I was compelled to have a unique discussion about spirituality with a friend of mine. During this discussion, I came to the understanding that I had a psychic reading by someone who was actually dishonest and fraudulently conducting a reading. This came as a great shock to me, as this person was one of my pedestal people! Through the process of the discussion, I realised that my pedestal people were really like me and everyone else. But what was occurring in them was that they had the belief and the confidence that they could connect with the spirit world and it seemed that I lacked this belief and confidence. I became angry and disillusioned, but at the same time empowered. I looked at all of those people that were doing psychic readings and decided, right, I am going to do that! I then called upon spirit and asked for help with my self-esteem and confidence. During this period I became emotional, crying, shouting, screaming as these feelings ran deep in my psyche. The pre-menopausal hormones were also adding to the drama in synchronisation.

The next day I decided to go to a talk at an East London bookshop. A well renowned woman delivered a speech from her book about an Alien species. Stating that Aliens can communicate with humans. She was confident and put her point across well, whether she was believed or not. With all of this talk I became angry with myself again. Angry again for not having the confidence and holding myself back. In the wind of this turmoil, the energy of determination came over me. I then pronounced that:

I am going to speak to the Gods, the Spirits and all the positive beings that I could speak to. I am going to request an answer and solution to my difficulties and predicaments at this time. I shall speak to all I have to speak to, to attain my goal and empower others too!

It dawned on me, that there is not only one way to speak to the spiritual world but there are many ways. At that point, I really began to consider what was happening for and to us humans on planet earth at this time. My analysis was that our minds are stopping us from really being the Divine spirits of who we could be. The thoughts in my mind were an example of this. These thoughts carrying messages and seeds of doubt and fear can stop our advancement. It came to me in a flash.

MEDITATION! Slow your thoughts down and listen to the voice within. Of course my next action was to meditate. Months of this on-going meditation then inspired me to produce my own guided DNA Activation Meditation CD. The purpose of this CD was to awaken the whole body to greatness by the process of externally speaking words aimed to re-programme the internal cells within the body to wellness.

I am not sure where this energy came from but determination led me to produce it and then go into the studio to record my voice. I sat for fifty minutes and channelled this CD, and why?

Because I believed in myself and allowed my Divine light to shine! Most importantly I slayed the dragon of self-doubt!

When my partner and I sat and listened to the DNA, CD we were blown away. After the fifty-minute meditation, we were shaking because the vibration and the power of it had lifted within both of us. When I listened to my own meditation I felt empowered to go on to produce more. Prior to the CD production I called on my guides for spiritual assistance. I then started to open up, mentally and physically relax. During this process, what actually happened was that my vibration started to shift. The shift then propelled us on to meditate every single day for three weeks.

The meditation allowed me to feel at ease with myself and the next month, I decided that I was going to produce my own self-empowerment cards that had an Caribbean/African flair. Again, I became annoyed and angry that most of the cards on the market did not reflect my world or me. Thus I felt uneasy relating to them and not able to conduct readings. After pondering for a while as to what to do, I carried on my process of mediation and asking for spirit guidance. A few sessions later, I heard…

"Go on, do your own cards reflecting images and symbols from the African and Caribbean world?" Wow can I really produce my own cards? I started with little cardboard square pieces with words and no images.

Giving others free readings with amazing and correct results. This, for me, was a sign that I was on the right road. I then went on to produce a template that lead to finding an artist and then leading to the production of my empowerment cards. For then on my mantra was that:

"I am going to believe in myself. I am going to believe in the spiritual world and Mother/Father Creator. I am going to ask them for information then write the messages I get or record them."

With my Empowerment cards, I was able to conduct successful readings for other people. I turned the negative thought patterns to a positive action and now, in 2015, I have a printed set of 44 beautifully designed cards. I have conducted accurate readings, selling my cards to the public and transforming the lives of others. As a bonus, I have now even gone further by co-organising and hosting a successful, self- empowerment and healing day attracting one hundred attendees. Most importantly and most powerful- this story is about, what I refer to as: the SHIFT.

The great shift occurs when you let go and say out aloud. "I am not having this anymore!" the great shift occurs when you declare that you are not putting up with certain things showing up and taking precedence in your life anymore. You are not putting up with the self-sabotaging thoughts. Changing the words,

I can't with I CAN.

Once you say those words the universe hears you. Your vibration changes and what transpires is a change occurs within you as you come into alignment with your destiny.

Use the force of anger and discontent to propel you forward to the positive and outstanding, outcome of change.

Connecting with the Divine!

The Mantra GOING FORWARD:
To propel you, you to say...
I AM GOING TO CONNECT WITH THE DIVINE.
What is inside of me, is inside of everyone else.
I believe in myself.
I believe that I can talk to the spirit of Mother/Father
Creator-creation spirit.
I believe that I can talk to any object in the universe.

When you use those affirmations internally, externally you will open up to hearing the words of spiritual beings. **All of us have the ability and can transform in this time.** My Meditation CDs, card readings and books intend to allow others to open up to their greatness. The products aim to assist people to heal and deal with some of the issues that plague them allowing the negatives to leave and the pain to go.

Letting the negative thoughts and feelings go, allowed me to look after myself. Letting things go, meant that I was able to realise that I can't expect anything from anyone no matter what I give. Another factor to consider in the process, is setting clear boundaries on your time so that you do not become resentful of others taking up your time.

Decide to raise your own vibration.

Create a space and the time for you to be yourself.
To nurture yourself to love yourself.
To empower yourself.
No one on the planet has the ability to do that for you.
You have to do that for yourself.
From your example others will follow.
It's time for everyone to look after himself or herself.
Everyone is on his or her own journey.

Chapter 1 Exercise:
Your Journey

☥ Consider what has drawn you to this book and what you hope to gain from reading it?

☥ What was the beginning of your journey?

☥ What did you learn from specific incidents in your own journey?

☥ Consider the negatives. What are your methods for transforming the negatives?

☥ Using your intuition, are there any times that you connect with the unseen/spirit world?

☥ Do you listen to your intuition? What in the physical world manifests when you listen to the voice within?

☥ Spend a few days listening to this voice and contemplate on how wise it is.

MY NAME IS NEFFY.
I AM HERE TO PROVIDE HUMOUR THOROUGH
OUT THE BOOK AND BRING A SMILE ON YOUR FACE!!

Chapter 2
FAMILY MATTERS

My Story

My life began in a small town in Darlington in the North of England. My mother and father came to England in the early sixties and I was born the year after the arrived. My father was born in Suriname (formally called Dutch Guyana). They both meet in Guyana, (which was a British colony at that time) in the late 1950s. The main influence in my life was my mother as she was the main caregiver. My father, a carpenter, went out to work long hours on the building site and came home late at night. So most of my time was spent at home with my mother until she went out to work as a nurse in the local hospital.

The maternal side of my family bore a large influence on my life even though I never met most of them. They were from a small village in Guyana, South America and hailed from a small family of mainly women. The real history of my mother's side of the family was unknown to me until one day my nephew came to me requesting information about our family. As I began to ask questions to family members, I found that there was so much that I did not know and to enquire felt like I was uncovering a bag of skeletons. Anyway, I went on to ask as much questions as I could from family members and in the asking, the social history of the Caribbean and Africa evolved. My family illustrated the legacy of enslavement and beyond.

My mother was very reluctant to talk about our history, as this would be a matter of shame for her. Even though this was the case, I still went on to do my own research and through my questioning what was revealed, was that after the inception of slavery, my family became a lineage of single mothers. My grandmother, my mother and my aunt all were unmarried parents poor and with little money. They all worked hard and for long hours. I was brought into this world with the same vibration.

My maternal grandfather, along with many of the men at that time, was married to another woman and had other women also. This situation from my grandmother's generation (circa late 1800s), right down until today, has continued in the family and created a legacy of embarrassment for them. In the small Guyanese village back in the 1900s, the community viewed an unmarried pregnancy as, 'bringing shame on the family'. I heard these words at various times in my childhood. The phrase... *"Don't let us down,"* was something that I heard constantly but did not comprehend the deep meaning behind it. All the pregnancies in my family, apart from one, were out of wedlock. This explained to me the unspoken pattern on my mother's side and the reaction of my family when they heard that I was pregnant without a ring on my finger. I was nineteen, young and at college with a part time job but I felt it was right, even though I was in an abusive relationship. To me, none of this mattered. My self-acceptance was so low. I settled for verbal, physical and psychological abuse and denied it by saying that, 'I loved him'. I had learnt about abuse, unconsciously from childhood and was repeating the same pattern. Living in a society that did not accept me as a valued member. The combination of racism and being overweight did not help me to accept myself with pride. Experiencing different forms of abuse, being bullied at school and at home and furthermore being a very quiet child, meant that I had a very low self-esteem. So of course with my esteem issues, I attracted a person who continued that tradition of abuse and it was a painful and lonely place to be. I never told anyone what I was experiencing, as I felt ashamed. At times I wanted to take my life and be out of the torture but having a child saved my life. I knew instinctively that I needed to be the best I could be for this little life coming into the world. He started my journey to self-discovery. I put up with the abusive marriage hoping for change until one day I found out that my husband had a child with another woman (maybe this was what my grandmother experienced). This, for me, was the ultimate embarrassment and the only way out was to apply for a divorce, which I conducted 25 years ago. I began to be myself from that point onwards...

The Healing Journey

During my healing journey I read many African American authors and was inspired with their willingness to express their journeys without the feeling of intense shame. From reading other authors' expression of pain, I felt that I was allowed to express my own pain and I began to realise and understand the harmful effects of internal negative emotions and the need for individual healing. I also began to acknowledge that the behaviour of others who are also in pain could affect the receiver of that behaviour internally and externally, leaving distressing and sometimes devastating consequences for the victim. I then started to look for a solution to this pain.

What do we do to relieve this experience?
How can we heal the generational pain?

From reading other biographies I began to see real examples of healing and a template for my own healing journey emerged. This began the journey to **forgive myself for what has happened and to forgive my family for their behaviour that I experienced.** Coming from an African Caribbean lineage, I feel we need to tell our stories and heal from this pain. I felt that my story needed to be expressed from my cultural and individual, point of view. The unspoken genetic repetition of many families history carries on and on, unknown to us, through a labyrinth of secrets and lies. This genetic repetition in Caribbean behavior i.e. our reaction to wealth, our hair, music, arts, self-esteem, confidence, economic power and money, goes right back to the times of our enslavement. I understood that much of my pain was inherited and that the abuse that I had felt in an unhappy marriage was my ex-husband expressing his pain and lashing out on me. Most abusers have been abused themselves. This is by no means an excuse for any kind of abuse but it begins to allow me to come to an understanding of what has happened in my life. It allowed me to forgive but not to forget what has happened and to stop blaming and holding on to incidents. So forgiveness is key to the development of each individual. Looking back and coming to terms with the incidents in my life allowed me to talk express and to heal.

My healing journey began with several years of personal counselling and various personal development courses. The inner pain of not feeling good enough for love, not feeling attractive enough, not intelligent enough just not enough! Took years to combat but the process created a path through my own experience, which led me to train as a counsellor. The combination of Counselling Training, counselling others and my own personal experience, has assisted me to realise that feelings of inadequacy and low self esteem run deep within individuals and society. We learn it when we are children. Our parents learn it when they were children and then they constantly tell us through, negative talk, behaviour and expressing that we are not good enough. These words run through our childhood leading to adulthood, which results in either constantly judging or being judged. This then becomes the norm and the language by which we speak. Society then goes on to tell us that to be Black and African is not good enough and the repetitious cycle is repeated. My theory is before we can go forward and heal we have to revisit the painful past. My conclusion is that the negative self-talk in the Caribbean community has hailed from the time of our enslavement when we were treated less than animals. The bad treatment and the sexualisation of our community still run deep in our DNA unnoticed and silent. The legacy carries on to this day with no organised structured defined plan of healing. This book is about my journey as a descendent of the many people who died in the African holocaust. I am affected by my ancestors journey and you may find that my story is similar to many others.

Today many of us suffer from low self-esteem and feeling unworthy. The words we speak, we carry and our internal self-talk carry negative vibrations. As Africans taken to the Caribbean and the Americas, we desperately need healing as the pain that resides in myself and in others is deep. This book is about my healing through the advice and wisdom from the spirit world. A major part of my healing and self-introspection is through meditation and this meditation helped me to develop my breathing, connect within and to listen to the words I repeatedly told myself. Meditation allowed me to contact my ancestors in the spirit world for advice and guidance. Meditation opened the door to the Divine connection with my MOTHER/FATHER GOD - THE SUPREME CREATOR. Meditation helped me to calm my mind and body down, which created a harmony and quietness, which, little by little, gave me the confidence to move on, analyse life and transform the negatives to a positive outcome. The process of writing this book has allowed me to heal even more pain; as for me this is an on-going process. Conversations with the spiritual world opened the door to words of the Divine spirits and my ancestors to create a healing regime for others and myself. The spiritual world has showed me the bigger picture and taught me to open my mind to another way of peaceful living on planet earth. This book is to be used as a guide for others to begin their healing process so that they can go on and heal the world. The journey begins within!

SHINE YOUR DIVINE LIGHT AND BEGIN THE JOURNEY OF SELF DISCOVERY AND HEALING.

Chapter 2 Exercise:
The Beginning

☥ What is your family's story?

☥ Look at the patterns in your life and your family.

☥ How do these patterns affect you?

☥ Consider healing the family lineage of negative vibrations.

☥ You can do this through meditation, visualisations, music, positive affirmations etc.

☥ Conduct regular visualisations of the words used by your family and imagine all your family members under a cloud of golden light. See each member healed from any negative vibrations and call for golden white light to surround you. Meditation can help you to heal.

Begin by breathing!

Moving on.... Who am I??

I find that it is very important for us to remember what has gone on before and those who have gone before. In this time of the fast paced 21st century, every advert and media focus seems to be on the future and new beginnings. Creating a society that equates newness with being 'good' and old things being frowned upon.

We have become a society where you always need to update things, which in turn leads to a very materialistic society. Looking back is not encouraged. Phrases like, "I am moving on," are used constantly but without looking back how can we go forward, I ask? As an African Caribbean woman, I cannot deny my past as my past is steeped in a history that is powerful. To ignore my history is to ignore a deep part of who I am as a human being.

This knowledge of the ancestral link considers, who am I?

This question is very significant in terms of forging an identity for me. As a child growing up in a place where I was a minority. Society and my ancestral history have affected my journey. As I come to the quest of discovering who I am, I search, as many people do, for my identity. Identity for me is closely linked to my self-esteem. Myself and others who are not indigenous to the land of where they were born, experience issues of integration and acceptance from the wider community leading to individual and community difficulties. These feelings of rejection and unworthiness can be exacerbated if the minority have had negative experiences. These experiences can affect their sense of self and then their notions of self-acceptance may be distorted.

Remembering of The Ancestors...

☥ This journey is a call to look at the ancestors. Those who have gone before us and those that have left their legacy. To ignore them and their input in society is to forget their contribution to each of our lives. Recognizing that they have paved the way for us to be here on planet earth is essential.

☥ Many of the ancestors have broken their backs to make this world what it is today and they have left their legacy for us to enjoy.

☥ I feel we must remember them and call on their spirits for guidance.

☥ Opening our ears and eyes to their words of wisdom.

☥ To recognize what has gone before, call upon your positive ancestors for assistance and healing. Realise that you are a part of them and they are a part of you.

☥ My story is about my realisation that my ancestors are a bigger part of my life than I know.

Chapter 3
HEALING THROUGH MEDITATION

Meditation is the doorway to the spirit world.

Changing your vibration through the process of meditation

We are asking you to realise that this book contains channelled information. In this process Neferatiti will be receiving messages from another source via meditation and quietening the mind down. Slowing and quieting your heart-beat allows you to connect with the Divine energy. What we realise is that human beings find it difficult to quiet the mind and not have words, ideas, thoughts coming through every second but what we are suggesting you do in this book is, to dissolve those thoughts whilst listening to guided meditation. The guided meditations take you away from the daily thoughts by distracting you with something else. In all the meditations that you will be doing you will need to decide on whether you need to sit or lie down. But whatever position you take, you have to make sure that you are relaxed and relaxation is important because if you are not relaxed, your mind will be on feelings of being uncomfortable.

Quietness of the mind will help you focus in the future and in the Now.

The quietness of the mind will help you focus; you will be able to live your life a lot more peacefully. You will be more relaxed and less stressed. It is our aim that we teach you this because in this way, you will clear your mind from the distress that you have on a daily basis and this distress affects every part of your body by creating physical and psychological problems with your body. So meditation for well-being is important.

In this book you will be looking at how to raise your consciousness of energy in the body. This can be done by breathing in air and taking it down into your stomach. Filling your stomach up with a full breathe of air. Your heart rate will begin to calm down and you will feel more relaxed. You need oxygen in your bodies and this oxygen is one of the vital elements for your life.

SO begin with an input of oxygen, 10 breathes to start with. Make sure your posture is right for you so that your feet are anchored visually to the ground. Imagine that your feet are the roots of a tree, bearing down to connect you to Mother Earth. These are the preliminary things that you need to meditate. Make sure you are in a quiet room, that you are warm enough and not too warm or too cold. Phones should be out of the room. There should be no distractions from your family members and friends, partners etc. This time is for you and most of all enjoy every single moment of this meditation because this meditation is your bliss.

This meditation practice will open your heart up to yourself and will allow you to hear the Divine words of your own spirit and soul. We thank you for reading this.

Stay Blessed MOTHER/FATHER GOD

Chapter 3 Exercise:
Meditation

Let's Meditate

Breathe in and out. Whilst breathing, let all of the worries and the cares fade away. This is a time to for you to connect within and to listen to the inner voice of the Divine connection- our creator Mother/ Father principle.

Breathe in and out ten times. On the last deep breath, see yourself, bathed in spiritual water. The water is emanating light and it sparkles of platinum and gold as it washes over you. You begin to feel calm as all of your worries fall down the drain into the water. As the water spirals down, the last of your worries fall, one by one. You begin to dry yourself and you notice you are in a beautiful forest lush with vegetation- beautiful flowers, pink, green, blue, white yellow, orange and violet. The colours are so bright and beautiful that you feel energised by them. Breathe in and out again as you take a moment to enjoy the colours.

Breathe in again and out. As you walk away, you are guided by a light, bright being. This light being shines through the trees guiding you. As you walk, you can hear the flowing of water. Still guided by the light being, you walk on. Your walking brings you to a stream and you now visualise the stream taking away your pains your sorrows downstream with it. As you sit beside the stream you hear a gentle voice- this voice is calm as it is your guide, your higher being, your creator (Or what you make it).

You then sit down as it is unclear what the voice is saying but as you focus you hear, "Welcome make yourself comfortable. You are a Divine Being and I am here to help you and to tell you that everything is working just as it should do for you.

You are here for a reason and this reason will make itself clear to you once you stop and listen within. I am always here to guide you. Believe in yourself and feel that you are one with the universe and all things. Find time in each day to connect with your inner world give yourself time to be the best you can be.

YOU ARE A DIVINE AND BEAUTIFUL BEING. REPEAT THAT TO YOURSELF. YOU ARE A DIVINE AND BEAUTIFUL BEING".

As you sit and hear these words, you feel uplifted. As you breathe again, you get up and walk and take small steps into the flowing water. As you hear the fresh sound of the water, it massages your fears and now your mind feels relaxed. You decide to walk for a few more steps in the flowing water. The water allows you feel even more relaxed and at one with nature. You then make your way out of the water; dry your feet as the sun is shining on your back. Then you see your guide or your Creator. You say, "Thank you" to your guide or Creator as you breathe in again and start the day in a positive mode.

Meditation by Neferatiti Ife

Chapter 4
YOUR INTERNAL SOUNDS

What you do not realise is that you are the ALCHEMINST
of your destiny, your life and your future.

I knew that I had to write this book but there was a real block.
I could channel and speak to the spirit world so easily but when it
came to me writing from my heart nothing would come. I became
frustrated but decided to listen to a podcast and then I fell asleep.
At 12am whilst in a deep sleep, I was interrupted by my 88-year-
old mother who suffers from dementia. She woke the whole house
up at 4am requesting to go to work, arguing shouting and putting
her work clothes on. She finally went back to sleep after several
attempts of coaxing.

Although I felt frustrated and very tired, I did not get angry this
time but I went back to listen the podcast. It was by an author
talking about the sound of the Creator and I wondered what that
would be like. With a back drop of an emotional week, where all
kinds of negative things were happening, I began to feel really
optimistic. The words from the podcast were very encouraging
which seemed somewhat very strange! The podcast then began to
transmit a beautiful meditation that was inspired by the Creator. It
was so soothing that I fell asleep again and at 6.30 am I awoke
again and picked up the computer in a relaxed daze. I then heard
an internal message that sounded really profound.

The words of the Creator speaking to me……

'Sound is the most essential element in creation.
You can change anything by your own internal words
and it was now for you to go ahead and do.'

Whilst listening to this, my mind shifted as suddenly, I felt the pain in my back; the monthly cycle reminding me that it was returning combined with the negativities of the last week the negative feelings were urging to come back and take over. In that instance the words that came to me were that:

Your internal sounds can transcend this. You are your own alchemist and you can change this. Just try and experiment and see what happens what have you to lose! This was the point, at which I said to myself, "I can change this world that I am in. I am going to transform my body and mind without any tablets. I am going to move beyond this pain. I am going to become an alchemist for myself as that would be the only example that I would understand."

Once I was able to speak those words repeatedly, the pain slowly but surely disappeared. My mind was willing and there was no doubt of, what I had to do. This experience would be a chapter in my own self-empowerment book. A book about the transformation of the Self, through the Self. The reasons why others, as well as myself, fight externally and internally is because we are in disharmony with the Self. The ego wants to rule using the mind as a vehicle. The word sound vibration are the wheels and the mechanism of which it runs. I am now to go into an experiment to see how I can transform the Self though words, music, sound and self-talk. Creating a transformation of Self into a light body. I told myself that, I will feel the negative vibrations of the pain, as I felt it was there to experienced. Feel it, breathe it, smell it, and after that, emerge from it transformed. I really felt the negatives and a little while later the pain subsided and a felt better and a lot more relaxed. My experiment was concluded later on that evening, my son, (the wise one) informed me, that during a conversation last night a woman at his work place told him:

*'YOU HAVE TO FEEL THE NEGATIVES, YOU CAN'T AVOID IT,
YOU MUST FEEL IT BUT AFTER THAT MOVE ON.'*

MOTHER FATHER GOD speaks...

Sound is very important; the very sound that you hear when you are being born is important. The very sound that you hear growing up as a child, the very vibration that you experience affects your well-being. Before you can speak, you experience a vibration in the womb from your mother. Children feel vibration, animals feel the vibration that you are oscillating. This vibration is the words and energy that you are carrying. This vibration is very crucial for the advancement of life's journey. Vibration is important in the transforming of Self because if your aim is to raise your vibration, you will need to transform your thoughts and your mind-set and believe that it can happen.

The dense word and energy vibration in this time is allowing humans to not be in synchronisation with the spiritual world and this is causing difficulties for humans. With open minds and on-going meditation, you will be able to connect with the spiritual world bringing in positivity. You begin with the intention of bringing light into your meditation. With this light, you will be assisted to lift your energy. Some communities have lifted the vibration of their whole community. They have done this through their own positive determination.

The vibration that we are now talking about is a sound vibration. You see in England, in the Western world and in many different places on planet Earth, the sounds are very dense and heavy. The negative thoughts and the negative words make up the whole vibration. They are being expressed through word. The word vibration in the mind is unseen but it affects the individual. Now the on-going negative expression creates vibrations in the individual and causes them to have a very low negative vibration.

This then leads them to become very tense and angry. This connection does not bring inner peace and goes on to create a lacking in the internal soul resulting in people not being on their life path. In essence, what we are calling for is for each human, through meditation and through the quietening of their mind to raise their own vibration and when that vibration is raised by every being, only then will the vibration of the society be raised and transformed.

The other planets in the universe, whom are aware of this phenomenon, have noticed the plight of planet earth. They know that thoughts can cause negative vibrations and the anger can result in the society being unable to evolve to a higher level resulting in the society being unable to experience peace and harmony. Individual vibration is so important and many do not realise the vibration of your thoughts are important when not openly expressed. That internal energy hits the individual whom it comes into contact with because they can feel it; they feel this energy and vibrations from others before they speak. Many humans can be telepathic if only they quieten down their minds then they will be able to tune in to what another is thinking and feeling. Humans often observe the body language, feel vibrations and look at how others are doing things. You can only do that objectively when you yourself are in a calm frame of mind when you, yourself become intuitive and when you, yourself are able to work on your vibration to connect within. All of this is very important and what we are calling for now is a connection with your Divine self. Connecting with your Divine self can assist you to raise your vibration.

INNER GUIDANCE

We are calling for each of you to have your own salvation to find your own inner guidance. Looking for guidance outside of the Self is an illusion. The guidance is from inside. If you look at very young children they have a very light vibration. They do not have the baggage of life and living. They are happy; their vibration is light. So this is the optimum vibration you can receive.

Once your vibration is light, you can hear the words and the guidance of the Almighty Creator. What we are calling for is for each of you to look at your mental and physical language on a daily basis. The sounds that you make, try to make the sounds positive. You are to look at the positives and the negatives and you are to go forward learning from these two polar positions, because these two things keep you in balance. Some people are positive, positive, positive and then one day the negative just pops up with a force because they have not actually acknowledged the experience of the negative vibration. Everything has come to you with a vibration and that vibration is to be experienced. If that vibration is very detrimental to you, you can protect yourself in a ball of light.

Ball of Light Visualisation.

Imagine a ball of golden light surrounding you, repelling the negatives.

Every individual need to get their vibrations balanced, like the scales of

MAAT (EGYPTIAN), (Representation of positive and negative)

Many of you, work hard without any breaks and some of you have too many breaks without any work. It is all about balance so you can go forward.

What are your internal sounds vibrating?

Is it a fast sound or is it a slow sound? You need to hear your voice and hear the balance in your voice this will determine where you are resonating. That voice resonance is your own unique vibration. When your sound is of a calm nature through meditation you can help others. Healing others can be achieved just through your words because your positive words are creating a vibration that hits the other person. When your words are not helpful, it affects the other person, causing negativity in them.

MOTHER /FATHER GOD

Raising the Planet's Vibration

We are calling for raising the vibration of every being so the planet can move forward. The rising of every individual vibration is hearing the inner voice and hearing what it has to say because your inner voice knows the truth and things that are untrue. Your inner voice knows what is for you and what is not for you and through hearing and connecting with your inner voice you will move forward and create balance for your planet

MOTHER/FATHER GOD

Chapter 4 Exercise:
Your own internal power

☥ Do you believe that you have the power to change your world? If not, consider this statement:

☥ You do have the power.

☥ You can change your world by changing your word vibration.

☥ Being mindful of your thoughts and how they affect others.

☥ Begin with meditation and deep breathing.

☥ Before you embark on slowing your thoughts down, write down all the negative thoughts that plague you daily.

Examples are:

☥ I am ugly
I am not good enough.
I need to change something before I can be happy.
Consider your daily thoughts and words and release the negative words!

Chapter 5
HOW MUSIC CAN HELP
YOU TO HEAL

In the process of writing this chapter on music, I came across quite a significant amount of evidence looking at the positive and healing benefits of listening to music. Research has shown that music can affect the whole brain in a beneficial way than no music at all. Music involves the using of the whole brain. It influences all cultures and assists humans to learn language, improves memory, focuses attention, helps with physical co-ordination and development.

Music is definitely important to my life and I need to hear it often as it creates a sense of relaxation and balance within my mind and body. I found that music has other physical benefits that sometimes we are really unaware of.

Music can heal the body and the mind. Research has illustrated that music acts as a positive pain relief to individuals experiencing pain. Music does this by relaxing the body and slowing down the breathing allowing the pain to calm down. Playing music every morning can lower an individual's blood pressure. The tempo and pace of the music has a calming effect on the heart helping it to work better. Scientists have also found that music can boost the immunity in the body by releasing positive emotions and the secretion of the immune boosting hormones.

Certain types of music can have an influence on the body and the mind in positive ways whilst other types of music or sound can affect people detrimentally. For example research has found that hearing someone speak on a mobile may become annoying for those who can hear it because they can only hear one part of the conversation. Certain types of music played in aggressive way can affect the person hearing it negatively.

Considering all of the available research, it may be advisable for each of us to become mindful of our choices in music and the affects it has on the mind, body and spirit. So, sound is very influential in the area of music. Be very aware of sound and its affect on you. When you are at your optimum vibration (regularly meditating), your hearing will be acute and you will hear many different sounds. By this time it is important to protect yourself from sounds that are not conducive to your well-being.

Leaving behind the negative sounds, we now call you to look at the things that make you happy in terms of sound. It might be certain instruments make you feel good; it might be they create positive sounds for you. You may need to surround your home and environment with beautiful sounds from nature i.e. flowing water or birds tweeting. These sounds can nurture you, creating a beautiful and relaxing environment in your home. This will counteract the influence of the outside world reflecting its sound, allowing you to feel balanced and contented in your home environment.

Whilst growing up and even today, I found and still find that music can be used to create movements for healing large amounts of people. For example Native and indigenous people use drumming for mediation and healing. Music can also illustrate what is going on in a specific environment and become influential in politics. There have been many songs made that have words that call for peace and love etc.
An example of this is during the 1960s, specific music was influential for creating and enhancing peace and a coming together of people to create change in communities.
Music can take you back into time, bring back memories (good and bad) and create an atmosphere for change (when used positively)

We have noticed that sound vibrations, for example music, that is created with an angry vibration, may cause you to become angry and violent when you listen to that music because the impact of the sound on your psyche may allow you to become the recipient of that vibration. When you watch a film that is negative, the negative vibrations from the screen and sound can affect you, unless you ask for some kind of protection from these vibrations.

When you indulge in video games that are of a negative vibration, the images and sounds can get into your mind-set and into your subconscious mind. These images and actions can control you, without you even knowing. That is why it is important to be very careful about what you experience in the external world. If it is negative you will feel that vibration in your body and your solar plexus (stomach area). If your stomach is wobbling, feeling queasy, sick and your heart is beating fast, this sound vibration is not good for you and you will learn from this negative experience that you need to get yourself back into balance. So now you need to counteract that with something positive; you may need to meditate to psychically clean yourself.

WE the Kemetians/Egyptians find the balance-MA'AT is important in our lives and we call for positive, calming music to raise our vibration to relax our bodies and minds and to heal us from the negative vibrations.

Kemetian Collective

QUICK Psychic Cleanse:
Breathe in and out ten times. Take whole, full breathes....

Imagine a colour- whatever resonates with you. This colour is coming towards you covering your whole body. Gently, it washes over you, cleaning your aura from this negative experience. Imagine all of the negative words, images falling from you and onto the floor. In an instant, it vanishes.

Imagine the colour covering your entire body covered with positivity from top to bottom and call in for positive energies to balance you.

Visualise yourself beaming with yellow sunshine light.

CHAPTER 5 Exercise:
Music vibration

☥ Look at ways in which you can use music to transform
and heal yourself.

☥ Consider spending a week researching soothing music to
help you relax.

☥ Create a soothing playlist.

☥ Check out music with positive words to assist your mood!

☥ Listen to sounds of nature, water flowing, drumming and
research how you feel.

☥ You may want to light a candle and have a lovely warm
bath. Play soothing music to help you relax.

☥ These on going musical experiences can assist you in the
healing process.

☥ Monitor how you feel during and after each experience.

Chapter 6
MORE VIBRATIONS

Now to talk about vibration again as we said from the very first inception of your birth there is a very strong vibration that is within you, your own unique vibration. Some of this vibration will be taken from your parents and from the very first encounter with earth that a human being has, they make a sound and that sound is vibration. Who you are is a vibration, your name is a vibration, what you think is a vibration, what you feel is a vibration and you are your own unique vibration which can be felt by others but it is not defined.

What meditation does is to use this vibration or you may call it energy, to connect with another energy i.e. God, the universe etc. So, if you are calling on a positive vibration and you meditate. You may get information from the Divine realms. If you are calling from/for a negative vibration you may receive negative information. You do have a choice. This vibration is unseen but you can feel it once you are calm and relaxed. You can feel the vibration of others through their words and through their energy field. Many people speak about auras which is important too, because your vibration vibrates into your aura and it vibrates at a certain colour, frequency and sound. No two people have the same colour or sound vibration and when you are meditating you are taking all of these things on. You are taking on the breathing which enhances your psychic element, you are taking on the oxygen which enhances your vibration. For example if you are very sad and you are breathing shallow then you may have a low vibration . If you are calm upright and connected with your Divine source then you will have a very high vibration with a special quality and in that state you will be able to connect with your guides and the Masters quite quickly because you are already in their vibration.

The one thing that humans find difficult to understand is that the spiritual world and the physical world are on two different vibrations. The vibration of the human body can be very dense, the thought state, the mind and some of the negativity pulls the human body in the axis of the earth. Once you are relaxed, meditating and lose the heavy vibration, you will be able to contact the beings in other worlds because your vibration would have been shifted. This process of meditation is free. There will be many who will try to stop you from meditating but tell them of the good things that can come out of it. Today we are helping you with the vibration and the energy. THANK YOU FOR READING OUR WORDS MOTHER/FATHER CREATOR AMEN RA!

Mantra:
"I call in violet light into my body, mind and soul to alleviate the negatives and to release me from the vibrational bond from the past."

CHAPTER 6 Exercise:
Sound vibrations

☥ Energy is a vibration and every living organism that has been created has a vibration.

☥ What sounds and vibrations did you hear and feel when you were a child from parents, school, family or adults around you?

☥ Do these words and feelings still affect you negatively or positively?

☥ Do you instinctively feel the vibrations of others? Acknowledge the vibrations the next time you are in a crowded environment. The journey begins within!

Chapter 7
LEARNING FROM NEGATIVITY AGAIN!

AYA = "fern"

SYMBOL OF ENDURANCE AND
RESOURCEFULNESSTHE FERN
IS A HARDY PLANT THAT CAN
GROW IN DIFFICULT PLACES.
"AN INDIVIDUAL WHO
WEARS THIS SYMBOL
SUGGESTS THAT HE HAS
ENDURED MANY ADVERSITIES
AND OUTLASTED MUCH
DIFFICULTY."
(WILLIS, THE ADINKRA DICTIONARY)

This chapter shows, in practical terms using real life examples, the impact and the necessity of the two polarities of the negative and positive.

It began with my tenant leaving in March 2012. You see, I based my only source of income on renting out my home and my only source of income (the tenant) decided to break my radiator, leave the house dirty and also take the income with her. I had a mortgage to pay and mounting bills! Yes I felt negative!!! The on going assistance to my dad to care for my elderly mum was taking its toll. Waking up several times in the night to calm her down was a nightly occurrence. With my own hormonal changes , there were lots of emotions flying around me and most of what I felt was out of my control! I began to feel frustrated and tired, with little sympathy from my partner who just wanted me to be happy. He shouted and said, "You are soooo negative!" This state went on for several weeks. For some relief, as usual, I put on my laptop and listened to the podcast of 'The Laws of Attraction', by Esther and Jerry Hicks based on the book 'Ask and It Is Given'.

I even went on to read affirmations, all to achieve a positive mind-set. I called on the Creator, my ancestors, more positive podcasts, meditations and music. I tried to warn everyone (especially my partner) that I may feel upset, down and depressed and so asked them to bear with me!!! I felt that no one was listening but for one beautiful woman that understood, as she had her mother, who was elderly and confused, staying with her and she, too felt equally challenged. She also understood the pits and falls of renting and the impact on the finances. This really helped- having someone who could understand and not make me feel wrong. I began to feel relaxed and listened to. When I was alone, I realised that the problem I had was that I felt like shit and was trying to mask it, avoid it and change it.

The negative experiences, listening to the positive podcasts and meditation created an unconscious healing and although I did not take immediate action, the positive words that I listened to assisted me to come to a further realisation. It dawned on me, that in order to be relieved of my situation. I just needed to accept it. I needed to be nice to myself, compassionate to myself and ignore any judgement imposed upon me by others. From that point I felt better and I started to let things go. As I looked in the mirror, I reminded myself to be gentle and to look after myself. I just decided to limit my time with those that couldn't bear the pain of hearing me.

I then began to come to the conclusion that what was occurring inside of me was that this negative moment in my life was my greatest lesson. It wasn't about being negative at all. The lesson at this time was about sharing and experiencing with others then using this experience as a tool for learning. The lesson taught me, most importantly, that there would always be times that are not necessarily happy, times where I would feel challenged, but what was important was how I dealt with those times and what strategies worked for me.

I could sit and write a fictional book about happiness and avoiding all negatives and tell people what they need to do and how to do it from a position of supreme power feeling that I am higher or more intelligent but that would give the readers no insight into how to deal with emotions and feelings that plague us. How do we to deal with high emotions at times when we are ill, mentally or physically or times when we feel alone anxious sad frustrated?

For me, I wanted time and space just to be who I am. I wanted a time and space where I could just feel depressed, alone and frustrated, a time and space to think without apologising and avoiding my feelings and I wanted a space where I was not constantly criticised for feeling. Yes, feeling an emotion.

This experience has taught me that we need **to feel the emotion and accept that we, as human beings, are both positive and negative energies. That the most negative the experience, the greater the learning**. The intense emotional pain and even physical pain can teach us how to be human, teach us humility for others who are suffering and mainly teach us about ourselves. The negativity reveals to us the real emotional pain that others are suffering and trying to deal with, the only way they can. The negativity can free us from the judgements we make about others about how they should or should not live their lives. The negativity can offer us ways of dealing with pain and frustration and when we find ways out of the pain, we are able to offer others solutions if they are ready. The negativity can be your greatest teacher of yourself if you allow it to be.

My realisation was that avoiding it manifested in a physical reaction. That on going avoidance had the potential of being internalised and becoming a physical illness. I say: let the emotion out. I am not saying to harm another or yourself, but find a safe way to let it out and express it.

I used the negatives as a learning tool to find out about myself and how I could survive through it. The greatest lesson was to be gentle with myself with compassion. Two hours after writing this chapter, my energy vibration had changed. I felt very positive and with this energy and vibrational change, a new tenant for my room turned up. Once I let go of the anger and stress, I allowed a new energy to come into my life.

What the universe was waiting for was for me to learn this lesson.

CHAPTER 7 Exercise:
Alleviating negative experiences

☥ This chapter considers words that we utter to ourselves at stressful moments. Whilst looking at your words look at your actions.

☥ Have you had an incident that has been negative and been able to transform it to positive?

☥ Look at negative incidents in your life. How can you transform them using meditation and changing your mind-set?

☥ Consider listening to your own words and thoughts that are expressed. If they are negative, can you change them?

☥ The negative experiences taught me to use my previously learnt skills i.e. meditation, listening to positive podcasts and talking to others. What skills have you used to counteract a negative experience?

☥ Can you use them now?

☥ From reading this chapter, you can now devise ways in which you can find your own healing strategies for dealing with negative experiences in your life.

☥ Consider people, books, talks or podcasts to assist you in your times of negativity and monitor your experience.

☥ Consider how your words affect others-negatively and positively.

☥ Explore the meditation on the next page for clearing negativity.

MEDITATIONS FOR CLEARING NEGATIVITY

Breathe in as you visualise yourself relaxed and at peace.

Breathe in as you allow all the thoughts to drop off and leave your mind. Breathe in again and take ten breaths. The silence creates a lower heart-beat, breathe in again and see how long you can hold your thoughts before another thought creeps in.

As you breathe in, see yourself filled with light. Declare this by saying, "I am filled up with light. The light beams out from me onto the world." The light is so bright that it beams out of you externally.

This internal light is your truth, your heart, your Divine and Godly self. Breathe and say the words:

"I am a pure reflection of the Divine Self. I walk with light and I oscillate at the highest vibration. I call on all the positive energy that I can. I leave my ego, negative energy, fears and thoughts behind. May this day be Divine as I walk and communicate from my heart, I speak my truth, as every perceived negative is an experience to learn and to change into a positive. Everything has two polarities positive and negative. As I go forth on this earth day, I ask for the gods, The Divine and my guides to be with me always.

I will check internally my actions and words as this day continues. I will oscillate at the highest Divine Godly vibration. I now call for my mind, body, soul and spirit to be full of light and positivity. Let this earth day commence."

Meditation by Neferatiti Ife

Chapter 8
External life affecting the internal:
The importance of Breathing Oxygen
for our vitality

Every human has been installed with the facility of connecting with themselves and others through breath. Breath is the rhythmic breathing in and out of oxygen. This oxygen assists you in your life and oxygen is what you need to live on planet earth. It is one of the essential items to live. The conversation today will be about breathing oxygen to transform your life. Before you do anything, take a big breath... breathing in slowly through your nostrils, filling up your stomach and your chest area and stomach with air. Then breathe out slowly. Do this several times. This rhythmic motion allows the oxygen to fill your red blood cells. The oxygen also allows your white blood cells and your plasma in the blood to work efficiently. The less oxygen you give the blood, the less it works properly. So you really are calling for the optimum increase of oxygen in your body and this helps your well -being. When you take big gulps of oxygen you will find that your heart rate will slow down. An example of this that I have seen in humans is when you become very anxious or have a panic attack or something fatalistic occurs, you automatically take a small volume of oxygen and say, "Oh my God!" or some other word. After that, the mind starts to tick and accelerate and you then take more very small breaths of oxygen. Now, the difficulty with small breaths of oxygen is that your mind starts to work very fast and your reasoning slows down. Your heart rate then speeds up, so your ability to think logically and your ability to connect with Divine wisdom is lessened by this very short and shallow breathing.

Now in terms of decision making meditation is very useful.
The main importance is to slow your heart rate down and slow your mind down. Now these two facilities work in tandem with each other. By slowing your heart rate and slowing your mind down,

you will be able to become wiser and you will also be able to connect with your inner sanctum. It would then be easier for you to connect with your guides, to connect with Divine wisdom because you are able to hear the words. This breathing in and out of air allows your mind to work at a certain vibration because when your mind is busy, bombarded with left and right brain things all the time, it cannot connect with anything else. There are then too many thoughts. A part of meditation and the main function of meditation is to slow your brain down, slow your thoughts down, and to take you away from the everyday struggles. Breathing well is the most essential part of meditation. It is essential because it allows you to connect with yourself.

Breath is your primordial instinct. It is the very first thing humans do upon arrival on planet earth. Upon the arrival and out of the womb, your own and your mother's breath are your first experiences before you make a sound. So breath and vibration are important and we would like to keep this very simple because the art of meditation is very simple and not complex. All we are calling for is rhythmic breathing. Breathe in air, hold your breath and then let it out. Use a lot of air to bring the breath in and then breathe out. Do this in a rhythmic sense. You can do this by listening to meditation CDs. You can meditate to music alone if you please, as there are no words in the music to distract you.

The functions of meditation is really to calm your heart down, to allow you to be relaxed, to alleviate the stresses, allowing you to have contact with the Divine world and your higher consciousness. Connection with your higher consciousness is the doorway to the spirit world and for this reason people will meditate.

This is the reason why I suppose you would have picked up this book. Meditation is very popular as many people strive for inner peace and quietness from the ever- stressful world.

Mother/Father God

Chapter 8 Exercise:
Changing your internal world

☥ Everything on planet earth and outside planet earth has a vibration. This is due to the molecules and the makeup of it.

☥ Through on-going meditation, you will be able to connect with the light beings in the spiritual world bringing positivity via the intention of bringing light into your meditation.

☥ Listen and reflect on the advice from the spirit world. A major part of my healing and self-introspection was meditation

☥ Meditation helps to calm your mind and body down. How has meditation helped you?

☥ Mediation creates harmony and quietness that, little by little, can give you the confidence to move on and analyse life.

☥ Meditation is the doorway to the spirit world.

☥ Quietness of the mind will help you focus in the future and in the Now. You will be able to live your life a lot more peacefully, more relaxed and less stressed.

☥ What we are calling for, is for each of you to look at your mental and physical language on a daily basis. The sounds that you make, try to make the sounds positive.

☥ Imagine a ball of light surrounding you repelling the negatives.

☥ How do you feel after meditation?

☥ Monitor and consider the above points.
Monitor your feelings after the Ball of light mantra!

☥ We are calling for a raising of the vibration of words of every being so the entire planet can move forward and the rising of that vibration is hearing the positive sound of the soul and your inner voice.

Chapter 9
Ancient Kemetian/Egyptian Guide
to Deal with Stress

My name is Arkenaton great King of Ancient Kemet (Egypt).
In my time we did not have the appliances that you all have.
From my realm it seems that you have so many things that you do
not know what to do with them. You don't know what choices to
make, as these things are all distractions from the inner connection.
You see, relaxation is what you call it but in Kemet we called it our
connection with our real selves. Why I decided to comment on
relaxation is because relaxation is so important to your Divine
being- physically, mentally, spiritually and for your soul. It is the
lynchpin of everything for you on planet earth.

This subject may take some time to explain but once you are
relaxed, you will be able to connect with the voice inside: your
Divine Self, your Divine force and the Creator energy.

To talk about it really means that we have to consider what would
happen if there was no relaxation. Now currently planet earth is
in a non-relaxation mode. You see everything you come into
contact with, including yourself, creates a vibration and you
feel it. If you sit quietly you can feel it, you can (actually) feel
your environment, once you are connected and relaxed.
Now the majority of human beings are operating on a level of
non-relaxation so their minds are running fast. The thought waves
are very fast and every moment is a thought. There is no
relaxation of the mind and humans will plan things to do for every
minute of the day. Now I am not saying that planning is no good
but what I am saying, is that you need to have time where you
experience the Now!

To experience what is going on in the moment, you need to have time to appreciate your environment. You need to have time to breathe the breath of oxygen. You need to have time to connect with yourself. You need to have time where the thoughts dissipate and in that time you have created, you will feel the vibration and connectedness of your own soul. Slowing things down.

What is occurring in this time is a disconnection with your soul and its vibration. If your mind is in charge, your mind will rule your life, your spirit and your soul. You will do things on solely a physical level and you will be disconnected from the other human beings. Your self-growth will be stunted which will result in wars, killings and selfishness. What occurs is people being mean. What occurs is people concentrating on themselves.

No, this kind of environment is very destructive and in the end it will destroy the earth and bring the universe down with it. So this is why relaxation is important. Relaxation through quietness and through breathing of meditation. Through on going relaxation, you will experience the oneness you have to every human being and everything on planet earth. Every plant, every insect, every animal and every word spoken. You will realise your connectedness and as you hear the heartbeat, your own heartbeat. You will hear the heartbeat of others and you will feel their vibration. If you are not of the same vibration, there will be discordance, destabilisation and that is what people are experiencing now.

King Arkenaton

King Arkenaton was a Pharaoh of the Eighteenth dynasty of Kemet/Egypt who ruled for 17 years and his date of death is unknown. Arkenaton was the first King to abolish the traditional religious rites of Egypt/Kemet and instituted the first known monotheistic state religion into the world.

What the future of planet earth could be!

Imagine if your own planet was on the vibration of peace and harmony and connectedness with the Creator. Could you imagine what kind of universe this would be? Planet earth's vibration would rise. All of your earthquakes, volcanoes, discordance with the sea and the land would cease. The raping of the land would stop. To be in the vibration with your environment you need to have time to appreciate your environment. You need to have time to breathe the breath of oxygen. You need to have time to connect with yourself. You need to have time where the thoughts dissipate and in that time you have created, you will feel the vibration and connectedness of your own soul.

Kemet (Egypt) and Relaxation: How did the Kemetians relax?

You see in our time, in ancient Kemet, we had to relax. First of all it was very hot and the sun gives us another vibration. You had to connect with that internal/external energy of the Sun Rays blasting on you early in the morning with its force. You had to give up every essence in your body to Sun RA (the sun). Feeling its vibration coming into you from your third eye and your crown chakra. We would sit, Nefertiti (my wife) and my family and absorb this energy and in that time it would take us on journeys to different lands: to the future and into the past and all over the universe. We had interesting experiences. Many are not documented. We would go forth with our visions and create what we were told to. We would connect with the spirit world and call on them for advice. You see through relaxation you could contact the spirit world. The process of man contacting the spirit world has been going on for centuries and centuries and centuries. When people turn their noses up to the spirit world, it is because they have been indoctrinated with the idea that this should not be done.

SPIRITUALITY AND RELAXATION

You cannot live a physical life alone, you are spirit and one day you will return to the spiritual world. So you are just one spirit connecting to another spirit and this is the process of the life after (the afterlife as you call it now). We called it the life after because this process is where you go on and learn life's lessons and then come back to the spirit world. Some of you return as guides in the spirit world, to humans in the physical world. Guides are called upon at a time when someone needs guidance.

There are times when we all need guidance. So this concept of which I am sharing with you is a completely different aspect on relaxation. Not the aspect that you see in the physical world telling you to.

'RELAX IT WILL MAKE YOU FEEL BETTER- la la la'.

This is the deep connection with the spiritual world, relaxation through meditation. Once you relax and meditate long enough you begin to talk and hear the words of your guides, your angels and your ancestors. You will hear the words, most of all, of the Creator of the whole entire universe. Now that is a beautiful gift to be given. What we are showing is a different way of being. What is now occurring is that the mind is showing you deadlines and things to do, planning, writing, thinking and none of this brings you joy. It may bring momentary happiness, but none of this brings a deep internal/eternal connection with the Divine source- the Divine joy and contentedness in your heart.

LACK OF SPIRITUAL CONNECTION

Due to this lack of relaxation you are feeling discontented. You are not contented with who you are and what you are in this time. In the physical world materialism is ruling and, in your time, you are all wanting to change things to make things better. Your minds are full of things, how to look better; how to talk better; how to do this better; how to do that better. None of it is about the connection with yourselves, in your heart, in your soul and in your mind. I am screaming from the spirit world for humans to elevate themselves through a relaxation of the mind, body and soul.

RELAXATION RITUAL

You all need to connect with you inner hearts, feel the thumping heartbeat. Listen to it. Block out any other sounds and listen to your heartbeat. Listen to all we have to say. Listen to your own Divine will! LISTEN! Say to your mind: QUIET, QUIET and keep repeating that word. Find a time in the day when you say QUIET.

QUIET

Everything goes off-the computer, the TV and the music. Sit in a room, burn some incense, light some candles; this is your time where everything from the physical world gets silenced. It does not matter how you look, how big you are, how small you are, how big your feet are blah blah blah! We hear it in the spirit world, we hear it, we hear your minds ticking, ticking, ticking thoughts of the physical and the materialism. We are asking each one of you every single one of you humans to put the physical world at bay every day and ask yourselves:

What can I do for my fellow human being?

How can I help the collective consciousness to raise the vibration of this planet?

Whether you believe in these words, feel the vibration of what I am saying. I'm asking every single one of you to save this planet. We (the spirit world) are asking every single one of you to think about your fellow man and what you can do. There are so many beings on this planet thinking about them selves and we are tired of this monotonous thinking.

'What should I put on today? Ooh I look nice in this. Ooh what should I buy? Ooh where should I go?' You will not find happiness in all of these things that you are doing and this is why some of you decide to take drugs; some of you decide to drink alcohol because inside you are not happy. There are many ways to find happiness. What we are offering you from the spiritual world is one way. This way today is through relaxation.

Your Life is yours and nobody else's and so through relaxation on a daily basis you will come to this inner happiness. The inner happiness is what it is like to be relaxed. Now to explain and to assist you to become relaxed: The first thing you need to do once you say 'relax' is to, BREATHE IN…. and that is the beginning of relaxation and before you go through the breathing try to adjust your mind, make yourself comfortable try not to allow your mind to consider all the things that you have to do.

Consider what it is you could be grateful for, in this time. This is called gratitude.

GRATITUDE

Be grateful for being able to hear. If you can already hear, if you can breathe- be grateful that you can breathe independently. If you can walk, be grateful that you can walk independently. If you can speak, be grateful that you can speak independently. Breathe these words in and out.

Visualise the universe and say:

"I am grateful for all of the things that the Creator has given me".

Whether you are meditating or whether you are lying down or walking...whatever mode of relaxation you chose it is up to you. Sitting down and lying down will assist you to relax even more. So while you relax you see the word RELAX, RELAX, RELAX and imagine all of your problems and worries float away. Relaxation is about breathing deeply in and out. Repeatedly, breathe in and breathe out, taking deep breaths. Continue to breathe in this fashion until you feel all the worries slipping away because this will be a ritual that you have carved out for yourself on a daily basis. Do this on a daily basis; it doesn't matter how long it is. Every worry, every idea is kept at bay and you concentrate on just breathing deeply.

Conquer all of the thoughts as you focus on gratitude. You see what is happening in your body is that the oxygen is going to your red blood cells, your white blood cells and your platelets. The oxygen is going into your chest, going into your stomach, into your internal organs and is slowing the heartbeat down allowing the body to relax. This puts less pressure on the heart because stress allows the heart to pump faster and makes your brain cells work faster causing headaches, an increased heart rate, stress to the body and high blood pressure. It has been shown in your time, that non-relaxation and breathing fast, being in a stressful life, induces different kinds of illness. So we are going to do the absolute opposite to breathing fast:

Arkenaton's three minute meditation:

Say to yourself…"I am going to slow my breathing down, allowing all the oxygen to go to different parts of my body by deep breathing and as I breathe in deeply, filling up my stomach with air, I visualise the oxygen running to assist all the organs of my body, slowing everything down connecting me with my internal being. Any aches and pains I see slide away in this moment and I visualise myself floating on a cloud. All the relaxation is coming and as I sit on this cloud, I will feel more and more at ease. The more I feel at ease, the more I will be creating an energy connecting with the Divine Being of who I am."

Arkenaton continues…

I have come through from the spiritual world to tell you that I am not ramping today because this is serious times. I am coming forth with a force and energy to move this land on, before it creates its own demise. I am calling for the essence of relaxation to be within every being in this planet. You can see things are crumbling in the modern world; everything that has been in the darkness is coming into the light. The truth is coming out; things are changing; the world is changing and you are a part of that change. Do not see yourself as an insignificant being. That is why the essence of relaxation is important and we really call this relaxation as a connection with the Divine being of who you are. Who are you really? Do not be afraid of those words, WHO AM I? ask yourself as you are relaxing ask yourself those words as you are taking time to be with oneself. This is the most important time of your day. Whatever you are doing the most important time of your day is now and hear this again:

THE MOST IMPORTANT TIME OF THE DAY IS THE TIME
WHEN YOU ARE RELAXED AND AT ONE WITH YOURSELF.

Through oneself you will find your higher being, your higher place,
and the time for you to give yourself the energy to move on.

**Going back into history. In the times of great Kemet.
How did they create the great monuments?**

We knew that if we did not take time in every single earth day as the
sun arises up to connect and to be at one with our surroundings,
that we could not create what we have now created. We are saying
to mankind, that you have the ability to do and create the
monuments and the pyramids that we have created. The only way
you can create is to move your vibration up from its dense place.
To move your vibration from the dense place now, to create
and manifest, you would need to stop every single day and relax.
We call this relaxation time- A connection with the Divine and your
Higher Self. Through that daily connection, you will be able to
function better in your physical world. This is an issue that has
gone far beyond race, culture and creed. We are now in a time
where we have to get the vibration of each human being on a
certain level so they can see past race, culture and creed and so
they can see past prejudices. You are all one energy vibrating at
different vibrations, you are just being housed in different human
bodies. Each one of you need to remove those value systems as
they only create prejudices. We had these prejudices in ancient
Egypt/Kemet and with all the different vibrations that came into
our land, we had to make sure that we were self-confident.

Relaxation for us (and now still is) the most important and fundamental element of every single man on the planet earth. When the beings on planet earth raise their vibration, they will create one harmonic vibration with each other. Planet earth will then heal and become a Powerful place. Race, creed or religious prejudices will be eradicated. It is now for every single being to move away from the selfish material world to raise the vibration of this planet so the animals will feel better and the environment will become healthier. The whole universe will view earth as an example of a planet that has moved on from the dense, negative, vibration. As you know, in my time we had all the different religions coming into our land.

When I saw this, I said, "NO!"
One religion-we made it simple-I want peace in this land.
I am about peace and I see relaxation as peace;
Peace with your mind,
Peace with your soul
Peace with your spirit
Peace with your fellow man.

Today I am glad that Neferatiti had decided to do this book because not many people are vibrating on a positive level, as it is not easy to connect with the spirits and the positive energies in the universe. Those of us that are on the highest echelons in the spirit world know that it is not easy to vibrate on a positive level. The level that is needed for positivity would mean that you would need to clear a lot of the internal negatives. You have to be an open minded being to know that there are many planets out there oscillating different energies.

When I speak I have my own spirits coming through as well. That is why you can, 'Feel the Force' (as they say in the film Star Wars) that my voice is vibrating in this time. Although we are in the spiritual world, we see the physical world too. We pick up on things, we are not blinded, but anyway the comment on the Star Wars the film is a bit of humour.

What I am saying on this day on the subject of relaxation is to take time each of you to relax so that your vibration can shift. Give yourself that time for Soothing music and quietness. Turn all the electrics off. Soothe your mind. Go in the bath -do what you have to do. You know what is right for you.

RELAXATION TIPS

Take time to connect to the energy of what you are. Relaxation is important so that you can be who you are in this time. You know who you are! Take time to sit down and connect with who you are. What is your passion? What do you feel you are in this time? Ask yourself these questions and do not be afraid of the answer. If the answers are negative, bring a positive energy to clear that. Through your word vibrations, call in for positive energy. Say:

"I want to transmute this- I want to move this- I want to change this negative to positive -I want to see a different way of being in this."

You can do it!

This time of relaxation is for you to grow into positivity for you to move beyond, "what shoes I am going to buy." Move beyond the minute thoughts on to greater things. Call upon the energy that you 'need' to develop as a powerful being. You are here on planet earth for a particular path. You may not know what it is but find your passion. The activity that you conduct easily will lead you to your path. Call on it and ask for a way to be made for you to follow your Divine path.

Call upon the Creator and say, "Creator, show me the way to find my path. Make the path open for me. Vibrate on what I need to do in this time on planet earth."

If you want to be a light worker then surround yourself with other positive light workers. If you want to be a healer surround yourself with healers. If you want to be a fantastic musician surround yourself with positive musicians. Connect yourself with whatever you want to manifest. Those words will create a vibration to lift your energy through relaxation of the mind. Relaxation is essentially breathing in and out…calming you down and moving towards oneness with the Divine Creator and your higher being. As I breathe out and in, out and in, my spirit will go back to the spirit world and I thank Neferatiti for allowing me to be the host. I am hoping that my words are listened to, as I will go back to the spiritual world until called again. I give thanks for this day; this is a momentous day on planet earth. That I have been able to talk and give my message to every single being has made it a momentous day. I can only call for the vibration to be lifted in this time, as it was lifted in our time. Amen RA and salutations to the sun.

"ALLEVIATING THE STRESSES"

CHAPTER 9 Exercise:
Alleviating the stresses

☥ Look at ways that you are stressed in your life.

☥ How do they stop you from enjoying your life?

☥ Look at the ways that the Great King Arkenaton and the ancient Kemetians relaxed and how can you adopt some of their techniques.

☥ Consider and conduct the exercises. How do you feel once you have done them?

☥ Consider the relaxation ritual and see how it helps you.

☥ Consider a sense of gratitude and look at all the ways that you can be grateful in your life.

☥ Consider ways in which you can relax:

☥ A hot bath, soothing music, meditation, deep breathing and yoga. Choose whatever suits you.

☥ Once you are in this relaxation mode then you may want to write down what you think or feel your life path is.

☥ Why are you on this planet and what are you here to do?

☥ This session is about relaxation.

Chapter 10
USING THE ELEMENTS FOR HEALING

Elements/Breathing

As humans we live very busy lives especially those of us who live in the inner cities of Western societies. We are constantly bombarded by other people's words, sounds and actions. Much of this infiltration I see is on the negative axis. There is constant noise pollution, mobile phones ringing, people busily speaking very loudly to overcome the noise from others, machines, motorbikes roaring and buzzing from computers etc. Moments of silence are rare. As I am writing this, I am observing the constant chatter and constant mechanical noise. I wonder how much inner reflection is going on in the society. This constant noise enharmonic can sometimes be aggressive, leaves little time for any relaxation and does not nurture your well -being. Hearing this constantly, means that it creates inner stress. As we increasingly become anxious and worried, this stress then translates into heavy and then shallow breathing. Our minds begin racing around worrying about money, clothes, relationships etc.

When do we have complete moments of silence to hear our heartbeat?

When do city dwellers have moments to hear and see natural running water and the waves? When do they get to smell the sea and witness the beauty that planet earth unveils?

We endure a lack of trees, birds, squirrels and a manner of other animals as we become disconnected from the natural world. The purpose of nature, as I see it, is for us to learn from it. It teaches us how be at one with ourselves as it is one with itself. The natural world requires humans to feel the peace and tranquillity that it emanates so that humans can give this energy back towards nature allowing it to flourish.

This invocation can be used to connect with the elements calling for a calming of the mind body and soul.

INVOCATION:

Play some relaxing natural sounds music and utter these words.

In this evening, this night, or this day I ask for the information, about the story of meditation in relation to water, in relation to air, in relation to the sun, in relation to the moon and in relation to the earth.

As we breathe in, taking the air through our nostrils, we become relaxed and I listen to the soothing music, allowing me to relax.

Greetings Neferatiti. I am the all, the everything and everything is me! I AM THE CREATOR!

Each and everyone of you are created to fulfil your destiny to shine your light and to open your hearts to love. All of this is done through quietening your mind, body, sprit and soul. Bringing in the air that I have provided for you.

OXYGEN

Breathe in and then breathe out. This unseen oxygen is what keeps your heart flowing and pumping. It's what keeps your body upright and what keeps your skin moist. This oxygen is needed for you to live and when you run out of this oxygen, your life on this planet will no longer continue in the physical world.

Breathe in this oxygen, as this is essential for everything you do in your life. When I talk about meditation, I talk about breathing in the vital air (oxygen). Every human is born to connect with this air and the more air in the body, the more oxygen in the blood vessels. Breathing in and out is humans' very first encounter with planet earth.

The first breath was air, which then, created a sound.

Oxygen was all around you and you embraced yourself into it. You understood that, the more oxygen in the body the better your body can work, the better you can speak, the better you can think and the better you can hear. The better you can play an instrument, the better you can sing.

The vibration and the sound becomes more harmonic with more oxygen. Oxygen is something that you need to live. The more oxygen the better for your body and mind. If you have a lack of oxygen, you can feel dizzy, you can feel ill and eventually it will stop your life. So oxygen is vital to your life. This is something that does not need many words. Breathe in and feel the benefits of your deep breath.

WATER

As you breathe we shall talk about water. Water is the other essential item in the process of transformation. Water has a primordial sound. The sound begins from the point at when you are in your mother's womb. Water around you allows you to feel comfortable. The sound of the water allows you to feel relaxed and the body is made up of much water, which means that you are able to relate to it well. Water is very important for you to drink when you are meditating as it allows the body the energy to have the vitality, to be able to listen without being dehydrated. Water carries many vibrations and it can carry the sound vibration from your voice. If your voice is calm and you are saying positive words, it will send out a sound vibration in the water and that vibration will affect the molecules in the water.

Water is very important and if you say something negative that sound will enter the water and that vibration will affect the water. When the waters of the sea come together, all of the ideas, and the knowledge of the centuries combined, are held in the water. The water holds fish and the plants and the vibration of all things naturally in it.

The vast water in the sea holds the vibration of the sun, the reflection of the skies and memories of the rain.

The water discusses with planet earth what to do next. You need this water to wash over you. When you apply water to your body the primordial instinct of the body is to be calm especially when it comes into contact with water. This water holds the vibration of waves, toing and flowing inside of it. Water allows humans to remember and connect with their time as an embryo in the womb; it activates the primordial instinctive feeling of safety in your DNA. This, in turn, wakes up the molecules in your body allowing you to feel the molecules of the water, creating a calming effect on your body and mind. This oxygen we spoke about is in the water too. The sound of flowing water is very relaxing for anybody that is meditating. It assists them to be calm; connecting with something that they may consciously or unconsciously know is inside of them.

THE SUN

Now we will go on to speak about the sun. The bright Sun Ra full of energy. The sun again can affect your moods. The sun is inside of you and when you connect with the sun, you can look up to the sun with your eyes closed and you will see many different colours and these colours will help you to move on and will help you to heal all of your aches and pains. Sun Ra will give you the energy that you are lacking. Sun Ra will tell you stories of the natural world, if only you will listen to her. She has many stories; Sun Ra has been connected to this planet from time immemorial. When this planet was first constructed, Sun Ra came with it to provide light, to provide energy and to assist you with vitamin D production in your bodies. Sun Ra is essential for your transformation of the Self, as it helps you to connect with the energy source and the power of this planet. When the sun is out, it creates a time of production and action. An energising time! A time to begin projects, a time to think and to be in the vibration of its energy.

Connecting with the sun assists you to go back into time and to find out your Divine connection with it. The connection with the sun helps each of you to realise that the sun is a part of you and you a part of it.

This connection helps you to feel at one with the universe and its elements bringing vitality and positivity from your interaction with it.

THE MOON

The Moon was created at the time of inception of planet Earth. The moon is at the side of the sun- the cool character allowing you to meditate and to calm your mind. When you meditate at the time of a full moon, the power of the moon will assist you to connect to the spirit world. The sun and the moon work in conjunction. I have created the sun for energy and for light, the moon for quiet relaxation and a connection with the other side of you. These two exist at the same time providing a balance and MAAT (Egyptian word for balance). We are calling for the sun, for the moon, for the water and for the oxygen. All of these things are needed in Transformation. When you are sitting down, you can connect to any one of these elements.

They will inspire you; they will give you their story. Trapped within the sun, there are many stories of other planets and also many stories of this planet.
The sun can see what is occurring in the daytime.

As the sun provides the light for which you can to see in the daytime, the moon provides the light for you to rest in the evening. Moon will see what has been done in the dark. The Moon energy and Sun Ra energy both work in conjunction with each other and within both we have the oxygen and the water. These will all help to provide assistance to live on Mother Earth.

When you meditate, you can connect with all of the elements and call for their guidance and wisdom. All of these things assist planet earth and planetary evolution. All of these elements help the trees to grow; all of these things help the animals to live. The combination of the oxygen, the water, the sun and the moon, are able to assist all the humans and animals to live in this land. I, Mother/Father God/ Creator, have put these elements on planet earth. Everything is interrelated- all working in conjunction with each other. Once you are connected to all of these elements you will be able to transform yourself and become a Divine Being.

I am Mother/Father God/ Creator; I am energy full of these elements. I am full of oxygen, light, dark, sun and the moon. As I am everything, I have positive and negative; all is within me. I am the creator of man on earth and many have looked for me but cannot find me because I am inside of each of you. Isn't it fascinating! If you only look inside of yourself you will find me. It is so simple and true.

MEDITATION

2 minute clearing of mind-elements meditation:

As you breathe in and out, you can connect with the elements. You connect with the sun, the moon, the sky, the trees, the animals and the stars. The elements make no demands on you as their calmness relaxes your mind. Imagine the vibration of the water as you visualise the waves. Breathe in and out as you see the sun rising. You become more and more relaxed as the moon brings calmness to your mind. Now you feel relaxed, connect with the moon, the sun, the water and the animals. Breathing in the oxygen will facilitate your mind to become relaxed.

The Creator, the spirit, the Mother/Father GOD- the everything GOD.

SALUTATIONS TO THE MOON AND THE SKY AND THE OXYGEN AND THE WATER

CHAPTER 10 Exercise:
To connect with the elements

☥ In this chapter we consider the elements: SUN, MOON, WATER AND SPIRIT.

☥ How do you relate to these elements and how do they help you in your life?

☥ Each element mentioned has healing powers and can assist you in the healing process.

☥ Breathe in, meditate and take in each element write down how you feel just focusing on each element.

☥ Sit in the moonlight. How do you feel?

☥ Appreciate the sunlight. What do you do when the sun is shining? Monitor your feelings.

☥ Bask in the waters of Mother Earth by swimming, sitting near a lake, sea or a river. Call on positive spirits to enhance your energy. Again monitor your internal reactions to the element of water.

☥ Although you cannot see spirit element, imagine what it would be like to be in contact with a positive spirit. This spirit can help you to calm your mind and connect with the external elements. Whilst engaging with the elements, monitor your feelings.

☥ Each element can tap into a different part of your psyche. Reflecting in the atmosphere of each of these elements can assist you to be calm and be at one with the environment, bringing relaxation and self-healing.

Chapter 11
Healing from Childhood
Word Vibrations

Not good enough (Revisited from a child's viewpoint).

From before we are born, even before conception, the words, **"Not good enough"** were the vibrations that many Africans/Caribbeans, were, and still are, subjected to. Due to this negative energy, many of us suffer from low self-esteem. Our parents, grandparents and ancestral lineage have carried this low vibration of lack and this has been passed on to us. Although in the days of the great Kemet (Egypt) we were a mighty people. The enslavement process broke us down and my own self-esteem went with it. The constant verbal berating from the slave master about us and to us, the shouting, the beating and the inhuman treatment has penetrated through the ages. I know you cannot blame slavery for everything, but because the African race has not inspected or healed from the enslavement/holocaust, it has created a legacy of internal pain, which has been passed down through the ages like an unconscious slow and deadly virus.

It is only until this age (50) that I have explored and examined the dialogue that takes place in many African and Caribbean homes. From my childhood experience, most of the dialogue is negative. The negative words that are said mirror the pain that individuals are feeling. We are feeling this internal pain in Western societies and that vibration leads to low self-esteem. I am not blaming the older generation or myself, but it is useful to come to an understanding that others, as well as myself, have experienced negative words since birth. Outside influences such as the media and the educational system play their own contributing role. Reinforcing the negative stereotypes of African and Caribbean children/people. Whilst in the womb, we hear negative words and then during our life times, we experience jealously, envy, bad talking, blaming and constantly looking outside at others for approval. We are always looking for recognition and when we do get the recognition, we are still not respected as we do not respect and honour ourselves. I am included in all of this.

In the past I constantly went on courses to, 'improve myself': healing courses, psychic courses, personal development courses, this course and that course. It was all to get that approval, that approval from someone and that someone, is usually a European. This feeling ran through the cells in my DNA and in many others: my grandmother's DNA and my mother's DNA.

Working for nothing and in low paid jobs did not help the self-esteem of my ancestors. They were left with feelings of being unworthy and inadequate and these feelings were often unconscious. These unconscious feelings, were powerful and expressed themselves in the behaviours, actions and words within the home. What is funny whilst considering this notion I began to understand, that unless I can heal and come to terms with this need for approval from the other I could never really be free from it.

It then came to me that: The most fundamental point of positive self-esteem, is to understand that the approval should come from within.

As a child at school, I experienced the negative talk from my teachers. They told me all I was fit to do was to work in a shop. Their words and behaviour were carried in my spirit, through my whole life unconsciously. So I went on to seek this approval. I felt that I needed the approval and it is only today, whilst writing this book, that this has been uncovered. My constant studying was to prove that they were wrong but also to constantly replay that lack or inner confidence and self-esteem.

In order to move ahead with our lives and to transform, we all have to re-live, be conscious and to heal our deadly demons. The words that attack us in the night, the words that we heard from our childhood and the words that said we were, 'NO GOOD' can only be replaced by positive words, **"I am more than Good enough, I am great"**. This means that our internal language is important. The vibration of words, we say to ourselves and others are important. Healing from the negative words uttered from others towards us is important too.

Believe in yourself by transforming those negative words and turning them around into a positive action. Every time someone makes a negative statement, neutralise it internally and create a positive action.

CHAPTER 11 Exercise:
Healing the negative vibrations of words

☥ Look at the vibration of the words creating energy in your childhood.

☥ What words/actions and behaviour occurred in your school/family/friends?

☥ What negative words affected you as a child and now dominate your mind and behaviour?

☥ Check out the positive actions and these behaviours can be used to go forward and excel.

☥ Empower yourself to move from those negative vibrations:

  • Identify the negative words
  • Replace them with positive words and affirmations.
  Examine them and allow them to leave your vibration.
  Become creative by writing your own affirmations to
  vrelease negativities.

For example...

☥ I am a reflection of the Divine Being. I shall not be affected by others' negative words and actions. From this day forward I will transform negative into positives and I walk with light always. May my aura beam with light deflecting the negatives away from me.

☥ Look at ways through meditation to heal from past negative words.

Chapter 12
MONEY - WHY AM I NOT
MANIFESTING FINANCALLY?

Allowing yourself to be completely free of your material constraints can change your life.

Although this book is about transformation, I have become increasingly aware that money is the result of much of the upset of the human mind. This upset mind can block the process of transformation. It appears to be a constant obsession with those of good mental health and those that are affected by mental health issues. This constant obsession is endorsed and upheld by the media and society as a whole. So many conversations I hear on the bus, the tube and people talking on mobiles are about money, money and money again. Money is the new GOD. Materialism has taken over and even some of the religious pastors are saying, "WHY CAN'T YOU BE RICH AND RELIGIOUS?" So as the congregation puts more and more money in the pots of the preacher's, the cycle continues. Most of the discussions about money are making people angry, anxious, fearful and upset, creating a cycle of unhappiness.

There is a common perception that if we are rich and successful then we will be happy. Even though evidence has shown, especially by the numbers of celebrities that have taken their own lives, that money and fame only brings momentary happiness. The constant drive to get money and spend it seems to be endless. Finally ask yourself. Is money blocking my transformation? You see the big hole in all of our hearts is being filled with material objects, which is the only way some us know how. We then crave for the next thing, and the next thing, never actually feeling relief or contented. The media endorses our actions by programming advertising that taps into our emotions, telling us to get the beautiful sofa, or the biggest TV, beautiful car etc as once we get them we will be at peace and contented.

What is the solution? The solution to me is love! What do you mean Love? I hear you saying. There is a human need, to be filled with love, contentment and happiness all the time. Many of us unconsciously fill the need for love with material objects.

On a deeper level, this need for inner contentment, once addressed, can change and leave our lives transformed and then maybe we can look at what we have, appreciate what we do have and begin to smell the flowers. To some, this all seems airy-fairy, but what most of us are missing is Love and happiness in our lives. No amount of cash can replace this feeling. Most of young people are completely bought by the media and its portrayal of money making you rich and therefore happy. T.V shows and the media, depicts people of a certain income rising to fame, perpetuating this notion of money equalling happiness.

Will there be an end to this? I really don't know but what I do know internally is that money, and the lack of it is a cycle and getting out of it takes a complete mind-shift. Letting go of the physical material world is one of the main goals of the transformational journey.

To transform and to move ahead of the, 'lack' mentality is simple and very revealing. Our notion and ideas about money come from our family and society. To move beyond this will call for an in-depth consideration. Starting with the statement:

"I can manifest my own financial freedom"

Begin to create abundance in your life by affirmations such as the one above and visualising yourself in an abundant financial situation.

Chapter 12 Exercise:
How to heal your relationship with money

☥ The exercise in this section will assist you to view your monetary situation in a positive light.

☥ Money seems to be at the point of every conversation.

☥ Begin with looking at your historical values on money i.e. how did your family view money and what ideas have you inherited from them?

☥ What views have you developed about money?

☥ What words do you use when you speak of money?

☥ Saying comments such as, 'I have no money,' brings a vibration of having no money and this literally comes true.

☥ Can you see yourself valuing money in a different way?

☥ Consider these actions to change your monetary situation

☥ Bring gratitude into your monetary situation and your life.

☥ Be grateful for what you have financially.

☥ Create a sense of giving away money. Once you do this action money will come back to you.

☥ Think positively about money by speaking positively about your situation. Say words such as...

☥ I do have money and I can manifest abundance.

☥ Consider ways to move on from your financial viewpoint by meditation, checking your internal views about money.

☥ VISUALISE YOURSELF BEING CONTENTED FINANCIALLY.

☥ Locate areas of abundance in your life and include a sense of gratitude for what you do have.

☥ Create abundance in your life by affirmations such as:

☥ I bring financial abundance in my life.
I live my life with gratitude and forgiveness.
My financial situation is now transformed.

☥ Now, visualise yourself in an abundant financial situation.

☥ Ask yourself if money is blocking your transformation.

☥ Lastly, research people with money. Examine their lives. Do you think they are happy?

Chapter 13
USING COLOURS AND SYMBOLS TO BRIGHTEN YOUR WORLD.

Meditating and lamenting with colours

Breathe in and out and listen to the words of the Kemetians. We are taking you to the land of Kemet/Egypt where you have visited. You have seen us stand bold and bright with instruction and focus. You have looked on our walls, you have seen the hieroglyphics, our pictures and our statements. We used these colours to depict how we looked and how we lived in the past. We will start with the colour purple and the Ankh. This symbol, this Ankh represents life. We are sending you this Ankh with a purple background. Purple is a colour of highest quality; it is a healing colour. It is a colour that transmutes healing energy. When you feel down or when you want assistance to speak into the spiritual world, you can zone into the colour purple and connect with the Ankh.

The Ankh is the key to the door of colour and the door of the Kemetians. We took the Ankh everywhere with us. It represented a symbol of life and a symbol of our protection. This is no mistake that the Ankh is used as a key. It is the key to another world and as you open that door with your Ankh, the colours are vibrant. The doors are open to every colour in the universe and every colour has its own vibration. You open this world to all the colours and the colours come towards you. You breathe in and out, keeping your heart rate calm. As you receive this information, we are to tell you what it means to have these colours in your life. The colours of red and orange are almost on the same vibratory level. They bring lots of action, happenings and movement. These two colours relate to the lower part of your body but they can also relate to headaches and an active mind.

Now this information we are bringing is unlike any other. Sometimes people have a hot head and we feel that the energy of this colour has then moved up from the base area to the head area.

Now if there is a part of your body that is in pain, it will register as red and orange. These colours are relative to pain, relating to the primordial instinctive feeling of pain in the body. You see red, is a very grounding colour; it is a colour that you can use to ground you, to keep your energy connected to the floor and to keep you balanced with the earth energy. In some countries the earth is red in colour.

Inside of the earth, the core is red flaming orange. Red with orange are both vital colours and they are the colours of autumn. As the seasons change, red and orange are indicators that there is to be a change. These colours are closely related to Mother Earth and brown is intertwined with these colours.

These colours are related to life in a physical sense.

The colour Black is also an earth colour. Black is related to the expansive feeling in outer space connecting with the skies and connecting with earth and the All That Is in the universe. All of the colours on earth and the Universe are a part of the one universal Creator. There is no single colour that is not a part of the universal Creator and all of the colours reflect nature. Look at the animal kingdom, they include and reflect all colours.

We now see the colour white, which is a base colour. It can be seen as a colour to lighten other colours. White can also be seen as the colour to heal you. It can be seen as a part of the sun-rays. Although the sun is yellow, it can also be seen as white.

White is also a part of the universe- look at the stars and at the moon. When the moon shines in the dark sky, it is a reflection of our universe. The white and black exist together in the sky in harmony. We here, in the spiritual world, hear man talk about the differences and the polarity. When we lie in our tombs our spirit looks up. We see the sky and the stars are white with a black background. The moon is white with a black background. Everything is connected in our world. We were not looking for distinctions and differences, as we knew that everything is connected and we praised the Creator for this connectedness.

We now look at the colour of yellow; the bright sun is yellow. This is connected with Sun RA and we worshipped this energy. We saw yellow as a positive, promising colour. A bright light calling us for healing, calling us for energy and calling us to go forward. We looked at the colour of green as the colour of the leaves on the trees, the colour of love, the colour of giving and the colour of growth. This is the colour of the grass; this colour is of all things that are good for you to eat. Green is a nurturing colour of nature and of a love for all things living and dying.

We look at the colour blue. It is the colour of the sea, reflecting the colour of the sky and we know that this is a relaxing colour; we know that this is a calming colour . This colour allows you to be yourself. This colour allows you to express your truth. We look at the colour of turquoise: the colour of green and blue- the colour of the sea. It is the colour of the water in the sea; both colours are a reflection of the sky… the beautiful sky that connects you with the ether.

Metallic colours such as silver and gold can be called for spiritual protection and spiritual connection. Every colour has its vibration and has its own function in this universe. What we are saying is that we use different colours for it's different properties.

We never say any colour is negative and we integrate all the colours in planet earth and the universe so that we can use them to move on and to progress spiritually. Whilst connecting with the spirits (when we were on planet earth), we visualised purple and gold colours. These colours allowed us to open our third eye, which then allowed us to connect to the sun and the moon. So, as you can see, the colours in the moon and the sun were the primary colours. These were the colours that influenced our nation. Sunrise and sunset were important to us and we integrated rituals of sunrise and sunset into our lives. We worked with nature and we were all very connected to our environment.

All of the colours had their place in our society. We found that the colours were magical. Meditating and lamenting with colours allowed us to move forward and we, the Kemetians, did things in order with the rising of the sun and the moon. Some of our monuments are aligned in certain places so that the sun, the moon and the sea, could be seen through the roof and the windows of the building. . An example of this is ABU SIMBEL (which is a place of very large monuments in Kemet/ Egypt). The positions of the monuments are aligned with the earth. This allows the individuals who dwell in them to be connected with the sun, the moon and the sea. While standing in the monument you could have a good view of the sun, the moon and the sea.

These three elements inspired us. We gained energy from the sea and the sun and rested when the moon was out. We used the moon energy for inner reflection and calmness. Looking into our internal world connected us with the universe because we felt that when moon energy was out, we could speak to other universes. We could see the beings in other planets and this expanse of the universe came alive in the fullness of the moon. We respected the full moon, as we knew that it was a powerful energy. It shone light into our hearts. When it was a full moon, we could hear the words of other beings in the universe: other beings and other planets. These were sacred times; we could then converse with these beings and share our knowledge with them.

Every colour had its own meaning as we have spoken about. All of the colours were used in our paintings. Some the colours have faded now but these colours were all a part of the universe and were all a part of the daily living that spurred us on. The golden light in our lives- this energy- was to give us power. It created its own God. The moon was a GODDESS and the sun was the GOD and these two elements worked in tandem with each other.

Kemetian Colour Exercises:

☥ We Kemetians were able to sit in front of the sun with our eyes closed. We could see all the colours of the rainbow.

☥ These colours allowed us to feel at one with our external world and they allowed healing within our bodies. We took these colours into our meditation, this allowed us to feel relaxed and contented. The colours of the natural world gave to us their venergy.

☥ The rainbow itself was a depiction of all the colours in the universe coming before you- connecting you to the natural world and its beautiful wonder. So there you see no colour is worthless.

☥ To create balance, you can visualise and connect with each of these colours and experience what these colours can create in your life. They create positivity when used in balance with each other.

☥ Spend a day focusing on each colour. For example, notice the green colour and how nature is green. How do you feel connecting with the colour and nature?

☥ Silently internalize and reflect on each colour and focus on how you feel doing this exercise?

☥ We are calling on the people of planet earth to bring more colour into their lives because a lack of colour can cause you to feel very down, very depressed and alone. We are calling for the integration of all of the colours in to your life. Wear these colours, show these colours - do not be afraid of them. Let them bring harmony into your life. We are calling for harmony in this time. We are calling for harmony of the colours and as you spend your days, you can have a particular colour for a particular day. So that you feel the energy of the colours and get to know what colours feel right for you. Each individual person responds differently to particular colours.

☥ The colour that feels right for them can assist them to go forward in life.

☥ If you do not want to wear bright colours, you can bring colours into your environment. To give you positivity, create calmness and allow you to connect with the universe.

☥ *When you chose a colour, you now know their meanings that we have given to you.

☥ We are the Kemetian collective, we say healing is important because we know in this time the entire universe is calling out for earth to raise its vibration using the connection with the colours and nature.

☥ This colour connection can raise your vibration and take you out of the thinking mode and into the free, relaxing, expanse of colour. In your meditation, see colour. In your real life, feel colour all around you. If you cannot see colour, you can feel colour especially when you wake up in the morning. See the bright colours waiting to greet you. See the colours and their powerful vibration speaking to you!

☥ We have come! A band of us, a band of energies have come together to educate. You have called a band of us, not one individual, but a group to come and educate those on planet earth. You are open to our words and you have faith in us and we are pleased. We will now be going back to our spiritual realm.

Kemetian collective from the spirit world.

113

CHAPTER 13 Exercise:
Colours and symbols:

♀ Consider the colours in your environment. How do they make you feel?

♀ Look at each colour and write down how you feel about each one.

♀ Consider the colours of your clothes and the external world.

♀ Visualise a colour that resonates to you and call for healing with that colour.

♀ Look at the symbols around you. Chose a symbol that you feel happy with. Using the colour and the symbol, breathe in and imagine the two elements healing all of your hurts and pain.

♀ Create a silent meditation facing the sun with your eyes closed. Imagine the colours healing you as you meditate.

♀ Do this for at least ten minutes. Write down how you feel afterwards.

Chapter 14
Attraction and the Laws of Relationships

During the writing of this book, I began to reflect on relationships in general, and relationships that I had experienced. It has been interesting to receive information from the spiritual world and to look back at my journey. My experiences were not of a happy story and, looking back retrospectively, I realise now that I had learnt to put others first in my intimate relationships. There was no manual to tell you how to relate. No manual to assist you to realise that you need to work on yourself before you are able to make wise choices of which individuals to bring in your life.

My challenges in my life were those of personal relationships. The themes were that I was always the victim and others were doing this or that to me. My intimate relationships journey began at least twenty-five years ago following the ending of a painful and bitter marriage. At sixteen, I began my first intimate relationship. I was still at school. We were together from school days; I became a mother and a wife at twenty years old, but this period was full of drama and emotion. The marriage lasted a total of eight years but duration of the relationship was twelve years. Unaware of what a healthy relationship was, I felt and was convinced that I was in love. During those twelve years, there were good, positive moments but my major concern was my experience of on-going, verbal , physical abuse and extra marital affairs on my ex-husband's part. Years of this treatment led to a complete loss of my self- confidence and self-esteem. After finding out that my husband fathered a child with another woman, I felt ashamed and disgusted- I applied for a divorce. The process of the divorce was painful but as time went by, I began to heal and once the pain subsided, I began to meet other men. I had no knowledge of what this would be like but launched into relating. The years went by, but the relationships did not last beyond two years. I just did not have much tolerance and if I experienced any problems I just ended the relationship.

During these years I just blamed the other person for the relationship not working, though I knew unconsciously that I had something to do with my failed relationships. Although I blamed others, something inside of me was propelling me to learn about myself and the journey began to be a fascinating one. Through discussions with other people, it appeared that other women and men were having similar problems in relationships. This accumulation of unsuccessful relationships, led me to the door of counselling and personal development groups, to find resolutions. I was inspired to ask the question:

Why are my relationships not working? Why are my friends and others relationships not working? What can I do to resolve this problem?

As time moved on, I came to the realisation that both parties, in relationships, carried unresolved issues from their childhood and also from previous relationships. Through greater introspection I found that I was carrying unresolved anger also. These unresolved issues came along with lack of self-knowledge and confidence.

My personal experience was a microcosm of what was happening in other relationships. I concluded that many of us trying to form relationships did so with good intentions but under the surface we harbour tremendous feelings of rejection, abandonment, denial, loss as well as the need to be loved, treasured and respected. Most of us are unaware that these feelings are within us and carried around as our own personal emotional database. Part of our own personal issues along with the others mentioned, is the lack of self -awareness and knowledge about how to clear these issues and not leave them dormant, subconsciously creating havoc in our conscious life. Most of us are unaware of the impact of relationships and of words that our caregivers said to us and the psychological impact that they leave us with. I had no formal way of understanding what was going on in my intimate relationships. What I instinctively began to realise was that I had to solve the mystery of and for myself...

With the acknowledgement of these emotions, I was adamant that I was going to resolve my problem, find my soul mate and walk hand in hand into the sunset. I was going to sort myself out! My plan of action was to attend as many personal development courses that I could afford. These courses enabled me to gain internal insight into my own unhappiness and thought patterns- which resulted in some personal progress. Unfortunately, after attending a number of these self-development courses, no major shift occurred. Puzzled and frustrated for an answer, I realised that there must be something more that I needed to explore. After some real soul searching, I realised that in all of my relationships the common denominator was ME!!

Horrible and painful as the realisation was at the time, the answer really was within me. This began my journey and search for a deeper spiritual understanding. It dawned on me that I had to gain control of my thought patterns before I could go on to find any kind of inner peace and calmness. In my search, I began to attend meditation classes. Meditation slowed my mind down, gave me confidence and allowed me to feel at one with myself, connecting with the voice within. With meditation, I was able to be more positive, clearing my mind from the historical negative words that I was plagued with. My curiosity began to develop further and I went on to attend psychic groups. I was overwhelmed with the information and my ability to feel at home within the psychic world. The psychic experiences gave me an insight to the inner world of intuition and the voice within.

My newly found knowledge was a gift to myself on my journey. I began to peel away at my emotional baggage and focus on nurturing myself. The voice within explained to me that I needed to love myself and give myself time to recover from the unresolved pain.

Single person's journey

My greatest self -discovery was when I experienced being single. I really exploited the single person's journey. I wanted to make it a positive experience. I firstly had my own single holiday. I took myself to Gran Canarias in Spain for five days and I thoroughly enjoyed the time. It allowed me to refocus my mind leaving much of the negatives behind. This time was concentrated on questions such as, 'Who am I?' and 'What qualities do I really want in a partner?'

I began to go on other outings alone and then included friends. I would have candle light dinners on my own. I would go for walks alone and listen to beautiful music alone. It really was a blissful experience. What this time of being a singleton really was about was enjoying my own space and vibration. It was about honouring who I was as a person. My singleton experience also included healthy food, exercise and meditation. After about six months of this lovely experience, I was ready and did meet my soul mate and we are together to this day. This relationship has also been about further spiritual, self-learning and development. I believe that without this self-healing and self-introspective time, it would of been difficult to meet anyone that was for my higher good.

CHAPTER 14 Exercise:
Relationships

☥ What is your relationship story? What are your thought patterns about relationships and do you feel happy with them?

☥ Have you healed from your past relationships?

☥ Consider ways in which you contributed to the relationship-positively and negatively.

☥ Consider ways in which you can heal from any pain you hold within your heart and mind.

☥ Once you have considered yourself and analysed your actions, try to think about positive aspects of relationships and visualise yourself happy in a relationship.

☥ Call in for healing of all the hurt you have experienced from others.

☥ Examples of ways of healing:
Meditation.
Counselling.
Speaking to friends.
Hands on/off healing.
Exercise.
Massage.
Healthy food.
Positive environment.

☥ The above may seem strange, but some of our most painful experiences are held in the body, creating illness and tension. These exercises provide ways for the feelings and emotions to be released out of the body.

I LOVE MYSELF! DON'T KNOW ABOUT YOU!

Chapter 15
Experiencing the Chakras
through Dance

Community Healing

It was only in my late 40s that I understood the relevance of chakras and the connection between chakras and dance. During that period of time, I found myself single. I felt that in order to meet people and to socialise, I would go out to parties and clubs as a way of reliving my youth. This time also provided an opportunity where we (my friend and I) could listen to good music that we enjoyed. Now hailing from South America and the Caribbean, we have a long cultural tradition of music and dance and this tradition influenced us.

At that time, many of us were unaware, that this music and dancing had a vital function for the community. This vital function was to create an opportunity for intimacy between the sexes. This intimacy consisted of a dance where you were held tightly by your partner, gyrating your lower body, causing your upper body and lower body to be connected with your dancing partner. Someone looking on would observe a hugging and swaying motion.

Growing up during the 1970s - this dancing was really a part of my youth. I was a teenager and I engaged in dancing with the opposite sex at school discos and teenage parties. This action brought the only non-verbal way that we could connect with another that was safe, away from our parent's strict upbringing and society's restrictions and rules. On reflection, the dance was important to establish a connection to the opposite sex on an energetic level. It was a safe and it made us feel good. We were sharing energies-these energies and auras were intertwining together. Creating the balancing of the male and female energy system within, allowing us to feel whole within ourselves. The dance was an action that touched us on a deep level. We were unconscious to this realisation- we just wanted more! On reflection, the close and intimate dance brought me to the conclusion that this action was a form of healing.

As a person from the African Caribbean community, I feel that there was, and still is, healing needed (especially in the area of our lower chakras.) The energy areas in our bodies that have been mentioned are called chakras. These chakras are defined as wheels of energy contained in the body.

What occurred to me, through research and my own observation, was that the area of our lower chakras stores a vast amount of historical pain from the time of slavery up until this current day. The constant abuse from the slave owners and rape of Black/ African women and men has been recorded into our DNA unconsciously.

What have we done with those experiences?
I believe that the abuse experienced has been stored in our genetics via the blood stream and then passed down through the generations unhealed. This genetic, energetic memory has created havoc in the bodies of Africans and may also account for the large numbers of African/Caribbean women with fibroids and gynaecological problems.

The African/Caribbean men, on the other hand, is affected in large numbers by prostate cancer and mental illness. Both physical and emotional illness may be partly due the systematic and relentless historical past of abuse. The enslavement process affected other areas of the body such as the throat and heart area also. The Africans were not allowed to talk to the slave owners and if they spoke out of turn they were physically and verbally abused.

The psychological and physical abuse during this period produced fear and negativity- verbally, physically and emotionally. The vibration of these negative feelings were held in the body and this negative energy of fear affected the area of the heart and the stomach. The heart and the stomach are the areas where emotions are stored in our body. These vibrations also energetically flowed through into our blood stream carrying these feelings and emotions into our blood cells.

Many of us are still affected by the negative energy of this historical abuse. The memories of those negative emotions are held in our bodies and they are passed down to our descendants. These energies hinder the ability for our chakras to flow and function effectively. Chakras in the body can and have, become blocked due to past emotions and physical incidents that have not been expressed or healed.

The history and process of enslavement has left a legacy of emotional negativity in the world. These blocked and unreleased, stagnant negative emotions have been carried down through the generations, they negatively affect the individuals and the wider community. There are and has been no programme of healing to deal with this generational pain. Resulting in a consciousness of, on-going denial that has then created a situation of destabilisation and illness in the African Caribbean body, mind and soul.

African/ Caribbeans historically used dance for entertainment but I feel the dance is an Unconscious Self-Imposed form of Healing. Although there has been no conscious system of organised healing I feel that the dance has provided an opportunity and space for moments of upliftment and healing.

Lets go back and look at the Chakras again....

Through the coming together of the two bodies in dancing, the throat, the heart and the lower chakras of the each person, creates an exchange of energies. The warm embrace experienced through hugging, releases some of the negative energies of the heart and the lower chakras promoting a feeling of healing and wellness. This is why some people report the experiences of, 'feeling good' after a night of dancing.

The energies created during, 'the dance embrace' taps back to our primordial kundalini energy (energy located in the base of the spine). These energies unconsciously remind us of very moment of inception (the fertilized egg and sperm coming together). Dancing and hugging, energetically allows us to physically and emotionally connect with another. We then begin to remember the time of bonding between the male and female energies: the very moment of creation. This dancing action creates opportunities for us to release some of the emotional stuck, hurt and pain. Further releasing of the negative energy, then allows the chakras to spin and thus creates energetic balance in the mind and body.

Our human need is for all of the chakras to be energised and healed, resulting in opportunities for African/Caribbean's and others to begin the healing process. The 'dancing experience' is one where individuals encounter, instinctive feelings of wholeness, being at one and to be loved in the arms of another. This loving feeling then advances to create a holistic opportunity to be at one with the self by providing an ambiance of well-being and contentedness.

Chapter 15 Chakras:

☥ Consider any patterns of illness in your lineage that may
   have affected your lower chakras

☥ Consider that your body holds pain and remembers the pain.

☥ Are there any areas in your body that is in pain?

☥ Is the ailment inherited?

☥ Have you experienced the feeling of being hugged?
   How does that make you feel?

☥ Do you dance or exercise?

☥ Journal your experiences.

☥ Check your body do you think that your chakras are not
   working properly?

☥ Consider healing though;
   Dancing.
   Meditation.
   Journaling.

☥ Call for healing in each chapter of this book and
   listen to a chakra healing meditation to bring you back
   into alignment.

Chapter 16
ATTRACTING LOVE

LET'S DISCUSS RELATIONSHIPS:
WHO AM I ATTRACTING AND WHY?

SPIRTUAL GUIDANCE

Breathe in and out - breathe in and out - breathe in and out.

The spirit of Mother/Father God, is here ......
Now readers you are to be taken onto a journey of education.
This education is very different to what you know already.
Many people feel that to attract someone in the love department
in their lives, they think that they need to dress differently and
that they need to look smart or that they need to put on perfume,
etc. etc. All these are physical things to occupy the mind. What we
are saying to those who are reading is these are physical things
and they may assist, but you need to ask yourself:

What do I want to attract in my life?
Who do I want to attract in my life?
Where do I want to go with this person?

We are convinced that if you are reading this chapter in this book
you are thinking about attracting someone of a serious nature,
someone of a soul mate quality. If this is the case, then your
energy will have to be at a certain level and this is not good or
bad, but your energy needs to be at a frequency that is of a
higher nature. This is because you want to attract someone of
a higher nature too. Someone who is oscillating at a higher
frequency than the materialistic, physical or purely sexual
frequency. To do this you have to be oscillating from that

frequency yourself. You will then be able to see this person and to be able to recognise that they are coming in your environment. You will need to be able to identify that this person is around you. You will need to identify the energy of this person and you will need to remove a vast amount of the physical attributes that you may have in your mind, as the criteria for meeting the perfect mate. These physical attributes ideas may be the very things that are blocking you from meeting someone who is your soul mate or someone who you may want to live with and work together in a spiritual union.

Now what we are saying is, that you need to find ways of going into a relaxing, meditative state. Sitting down and listening to good music to assist you to calm down and meditate is a good idea. These activities will assist you to clear your mind and to remove the baggage from your mind. You will then have a clearer focus. Once you have this focus, we are calling on you to work on your personality, creating positive thoughts, so that you raise your vibration. Once your vibration is raised, you will be at a level where through meditation and the clearing of your mind, you will be oscillating at a higher energetic vibration. The next thing to do is to alleviate some of the negative things in your mind about relationships. You may work on some of the negative ideas and thoughts through with a friend or a counsellor. What we are saying is that you need to move away from the self- defeating, sabotaging ideas that frequent your mind when this is done, positive results come into action. So this is a very deep, deep, work that needs to be done before you can become a person that vibrates on a higher level to attract your soul mate or somebody good for you.

What we are saying, is that you need to be of clear mind, free of all the negative debris….
Breathe in and out! Do this for ten times.
This oxygen allows you to think clearly.
Sit in a quiet space and ask yourself:

What do I want from a soul mate?
What qualities can I bring to a soul mate relationship?
What kind of personality must the perspective partner have and why?
How important is my spirituality to my relationship?
What is it I am asking the universe for?

Create a shopping list -but if your shopping list says, someone that is good looking, leaving out the other qualities, the person you attract may be good looking but not compatible with you. They may be good-looking but not faithful. So you need to be clear on what it is that you are asking for. Once you are clear, you need to look at your personality and try to be honest with yourself. Try to be clear with yourself about who you are as a person and why you feel that you want to bring love into your life. How will this love enhance your life?

Be very clear on the sort of person that will help you to grow spirituality.

Consider the sort of person that will blend into your social and family environment -the sort of person that can enhance your life and you can enhance theirs. Spiritually, physically, mentally. Mind body and soul.

Now to attract this person in your life, the secret is that you have to be oscillating on a balanced level in all of these areas. If you are not oscillating in balance in all of these areas, you will find it difficult to attract that somebody with a high vibration.

MOTHER/FATHER GOD

Chapter 16 Exercise:
Who am I attracting!

☥ Consider all the intimate relationships that you have had.

☥ Take time to lament on all of the one to one relationships that you have experienced and search for any patterns that have developed.

☥ Are there any similarities of situation or reoccurring personality types?

☥ Is there any negative feelings left within you from the relationships?

☥ Call for healing and forgiveness by using the meditations/ affirmations from previous chapters.

☥ Forgive yourself and the others and when you are ready, read the next chapter.

Chapter 17
HOW TO ATTRACT A SOULMATE

Through meditation, you will be able to bring forward good ideas for attracting a soul mate. We are saying, 'good' from the point of view that, for the individual, it would be very beneficial for their own well-being. What we are saying is that each day breathe in and out deeply. Slow your thoughts down- that is stage one and if you are breathing in and out you will be stabilising all of those negative thoughts. They will come to be obsolete because you will be getting your heart rate to slow down therefore getting your mind to think objectively.

Start with the body slowing down all of the thoughts, slowing down all of the words racing around in the mind and as we breathe in and out, it all slows down. Your heart beat slows down.

You will now be in a place of calmness; this is when you ask yourself. What do I need ? What qualities are good for me to have? How can I move forward and what things in my personality do I need to change?

Now this kind of introspection is difficult to do for oneself but through daily meditation this is possible. You may also decide to use your friends to express yourself. Through this process, you will be able to find out what is inside of you and you will be able to find out what is in your heart. You will be able to find out the truth about who you are. Part of this will be to dissect and to relive some of the relationships that you have been through. A part of this will be to forgive some of the things that have happened. For example: some of the things that you blame yourself for happening, some of the things that you feel have been imposed on you. This is why we say:

FORGIVE YOURSELF AND OTHERS

This forgiveness is necessary because without this forgiveness you may recreate all the events locked in your heart. Forgiveness is almost like what you on earth call, "a cleanse."

It is a cleansing of the body, cleansing of the mind and the heart and allowing yourself to be rid of all of the difficulties and worries which occupy your thoughts. In your mind, when you feel able to, and you feel that this is the right time, look at your list about yourself and consider ways of nurturing yourself. What could you do to be at one with yourself? When you are satisfied with looking and analysing, you can then look at how you can progress.

Look at your positives and your negatives, look at the energies of each of your relationship experiences.

Once you have looked at the items mentioned, you will be ready to look for someone of similar qualities as yourself. From considering and dissecting past relationships, you will analyse yourself better and know the kind of relationship that will help you grow as a person. You then will be able to find the kind of relationship that can help you heal your past pains.

In all of this, you need to open your heart to the person with all of these possibilities. You need to open your heart to yourself and you need to open you heart to love.

Many humans walk around feeling that they don't deserve a beautiful partner, a spiritual partner, a partner that can love them for who they are and what they are.

LOVE AFFIRMATIONS FOR SOULMATE ATTRACTION:

"Now believe and hear our words, believe in your heart with sincerity and say that I can be loved, I can feel love, I can experience love and I do deserve love."

SAY AGAIN....
"I deserve love and I deserve a soul mate. My soul union is for me to complete my task on planet earth and to realise that I am able to express love too."

Take the above affirmations and say them out loud and hold them in your heart. Repeat these words until you believe it!

Consider that:
You are able to be yourself without any kind of baggage stopping you. You are able to be clear the feelings of the bad relationships that you have had.

Say out aloud:
"I am able to heal from the ongoing pain that I have experienced from relationships."

How to Heal.
Now you may want to go through this process in meditation and you may decide in every meditation to reflect on:

Healing past relationships:
You can produce your own meditation on relationships and record your own voice. VISUALISE and play some gentle background music:

Visualise the image of an ex-partner. Go through the circumstances of the relationship leading to the break up. Whilst you are meditating, ask for guidance. You can do this with every partner that you have been with. If you have not had any partners use a parent/care giver. Through meditation you can ask yourself to be healed of all the memories that have been painful.

Call in for a band of light to come in from your feet chakras all the way up and through all of the chakras covering your whole body. Ask the light to heal you from this negative experience. `Repeat this exercise and when all of your body and all of your mind feels healed, you will then be ready to go forward. Furthermore, you will now be ready to change things in your life and to entertain someone of positive quality.

You can now identify the person that you want because you will now know who they are and what qualities they have. You should be able to feel your own vibration and at what level you are oscillating. When you meet that special soul mate, you will feel their vibration and you will feel relaxed and comfortable with them -like you have known them before. Their vibration and energy will be speaking to your vibration and energy. None of this is difficult unless your mind tells you that it is. Many of these things are in your minds because you have put them there. Say to yourself:

"From this day, I am to change my ideas about relationships and I am to transform ideas about relationships so anything that is difficult, or what I perceive as difficult, will be changed transformed and manifested to the positive."

This is a very simple exercise for those who would like to meet their soul mate and feel that it is their destiny to meet their soul mate. Let's go forward with another exercise:

Go into another meditation as before visualising your soul mate being in your vibration. This will put you in a good place to meet somebody. It is up to you whether you want to put a time limit on this or not. Be open and be receptive to prospective soul mates as soul mates may come in a different form to what you may already have in mind. You have to be very clear physically on what you will accept and what you won't accept. These ideas form a part of your criteria of what you need to go forward.

It is all about the manifesting of who you are and transforming yourself from the negative ideas that stop and block many relationships.

We wish you luck in your endeavors knowing that this is a very simple but effective method of attracting soul mate relationships. Amen RA Amen RA Amen RA

By Mother/Father God

Chapter 17 Exercise:
Looking within to create SELF EMPOWERMENT
TO ATTRACT A SOUL MATE

☥ Before you start, consider what you want in a mate.

☥ What do you want and why?

☥ Forgive yourself and forgive all of the others that you had relationships with.

☥ Allow yourself to heal.

☥ Be open to positivity.

☥ Be happy and contented with your single status. Keep yourself busy!`

☥ Write down and then consider activities that you can conduct alone.

☥ Is your heart ready to be open to love?

☥ Give yourself a healing from past personal relationships regime.

☥ Use this chapter as a part of your healing regime and await!

☥ Use affirmations and meditations to clear yourself from negative words and ideas.

☥ Be open to what the Universe brings!!

Chapter 18
LOVING SELF AND SELF ACCEPTANCE

A Kemetian Guide

Your people and all people on earth need assistance from the spirit world, to move on and to change your mindsets. We are waking up many in your world. You may not see them but we are waking them up- the ones of violet light. The ones with the special spiritual energy. Spiritual thoughts of those of light that can give a pure message to the humans in this time. Ok let us begin...

You see as Kemetians, we knew that without self-love, we could not be building a thing. We knew that self-love was essential to the very nature and nurture of our society. We knew that this was intrinsic to everything and by our production you can see where our mindset was. Now currently the African is not at this stage, not at the stage we were. You see what we understood and what our minds understood was that we had to make our own definition of who we were and what we were. Self-acceptance and the self-love is about the definition of who you are and who creates that definition for you. We were very clear that we would define ourselves. We would lead ourselves and we were the leaders of our own destiny. We followed no one! You see with this in mind, we were in the forefront; we were not getting advice from others, we were not waiting around to read others' books. We were the creators of our own destiny and our own existence! You see we are a collection of spirits from Kemet (Egypt). Kemetian is our word for this land and our spirits are of an African nature.

We want to be clear about this. We are from pure light; we are connected to Sun Ra the sun, the bright burning sun and no matter what religion or practice, we followed, we knew the sun was central to our lives. Whether we worshipped the gods or One God. The most influential things in our lives were the sun and the moon. Now we saw the sun as the day and the time for action providing the light and the moon was the time for connection with the gods or the one universal spirit Mother/Father energy.

We understood this instinctively and we would connect with the gods and the Universe in the evening. We had rituals at the same time, every evening. In our time, everything was very quiet in the evening...very quiet. We had no electricity as you have now, so people would settle down and rest at an early time, giving our minds time to rest bringing creativity to our existence, allowing us to be the best society in the spiritual world. We came together and left all of our fighting with each other, to create the energy of one spirit. We conducted this act in order to speak to you, as we know that your ears are open to us. You believe in us implicitly because of the knowledge that we have and the secrets that we have of which we share some with you.

The knowledge, if followed, can open the path to a whole new world. There are many important things to learn, but the most important thing, is self-belief. It can make or break you and we had that essential diamond self-belief, we had self- knowledge. Fortunately for us, we knew that this was the crystal to propel you forward as without self -belief and self- acceptance you will not propel forward. By self- belief we mean:

The acceptance of the Divine Self.

The acceptance that you are a part of the Divine plan.

The acceptance that you are a particle of the eternal God, the spirit the Divine, the Creator.

The acceptance that you are a spiritual and a physical being.

The acceptance that in your physical state it is very important to be connected with the spirits in the ethereal world for guidance and balance creating a balance in within you.

The acceptance and the knowledge that you define yourself!

The acceptance and the knowledge that you need a quiet time in your life.

MEDITATION
Self-Acceptance Visualisation:

Visualise:
A platinum golden violet light at the highest order producing positivity in your spirit. Imagine this light being drawn into your heart and your whole body. You are now a part of this light. Repelling all the negative energies inside and outside of you.

Turn your focus and attention inwards to look at the Self. Now self-acceptance is the belief that you are a DIVINE CREATION full of light.

Chapter 18 Exercise:
Self-acceptance

☥ Contemplate on this chapter and consider what you can adopt and adapt from the lives of the Kemetians.

☥ What principles can you use for your life to enhance yourself?

☥ Do you have quiet time?

☥ Are you in control of your own destiny?

☥ Practice the visualization mentioned and monitor your feelings afterwards.

☥ Whilst in meditation consider how you feel about yourself and look at ways to create a positive, acceptance of yourself. Did any negative words come up? Look at where these words have originated from and through positive self-talk change the negative words to positive ones.

☥ Writing the negative words down on a paper and burning the paper can help the words to be released from your psyche.

☥ Create an atmosphere of self -introspection. A time of relaxing and being at one with your own thoughts.

☥ You may want to construct a working tool to keep yourself positive on a longer-term basis: This can be done by creating an individual daily or weekly programme:

☥ Setting aside time just for you. This time is of individual taste but it can include -You tube videos, affirmations, meditations, reading, journaling, podcasts and relaxing music.

Chapter 19
EMPOWERMENT OF SELF

KEMETIAN EMPOWERMENT

We are the Kemetian collective. We are a group of spirits that have passed over from the time of ancient Egypt, our land Kemet. We refer to the land now called Egypt as Kemet as that is the name that we have given it. We feel that we are the originators of that land. We have come together as an energy mass to pass on some of our knowledge to planet earth through Neferatiti. Now as you read our information or hear it, we will first ask you to calm your minds down so that you are able to be receptive to what we are communicating in this time.

Let us now speak about Self-empowerment. Well to begin with, in Kemet, we worked very closely with each other on this subject as for us self-empowerment is very close to self- esteem. We had different words for all of these things because we spoke a different language. Our language was used to raise our vibration to the optimum of what we could be and this is what we called self-empowerment. Now, by reading these words that we have spoken, we are raising your vibration allowing you to be the best that you can be - in this time we are raising you to the highest level. To explain 'empowerment,' the word you see, to 'empower' is to give oneself power and not to give your power away to others. Many beings on planet earth in this time have given their individual power away to others. Many beings have given their power away without thinking and they become very unsettled, distressed and depressed because who they really are is not being manifested out into the world. What they are here to do in this time has not being manifested. We are calling on every human being to sit quietly with themselves. Whilst sitting the question should be:

WHO AM I? WHO ARE YOU?

Many minds are filled with thoughts that ground them in the physical world and in the practical world, but in the spiritual world, we need you to develop. Once this development occurs humans will feel a sense of balance in their lives. For the Kemetians, balance was very important. We thrived on this balance as we could see that, if we were out of balance we knew we had to go on to the next life and have to come back on earth again to learn our life lessons. So self-empowerment is very important and you can obtain this through meditation. Let us explain a bit more- it may be better to explain what self-empowerment is not. Many beings are being told what to do on a daily basis, hourly basis. Whether it is in their jobs or in their social lives. Whether they are with their family or with their friends, many beings are being told what to do. The main protagonists of this is the media, the television and the radio. You are told what to do unconsciously; what to say and what is appropriate and what is not appropriate depending on what society you live in. In the western world, the media is the force outside of yourself telling you what to be. The images are telling you what you should look like and what you should not look like. It is in the western world that certain images are put out all of the time and if you do not look like these images, you feel upset and abandoned by society as the other beings will tell you that you need to look a 'certain way.'

There is a lot of pressure for you to look in a, 'certain way', to speak in a, 'certain way' and to behave in a 'certain way.' People who fall out of that, 'certain' way are ostracised and seen as negative but today we are here to say: Allow yourself to be who you really are.

It would be useful each day, if you meditate and be at one with yourself.

To find the inner you and not what someone else is telling you to be.

You may need to move away from many of the outer things, as they keep you in a certain frame of mind. It is about you vibrating to your optimum spiritually, physically and emotionally.

Many of the beings on planet earth live in the past and do not live in the now. In the 'Now', where opportunities, ideas and information can be received. So we are calling for you to live in the 'Now', no matter what past you have had and no matter how sad you were. What we are asking, so that you can be empowered, is to leave the past in the past. Some of you may need to speak to a friend some of you may need counselling and some of you may need to go to somebody to talk and shed the past.

Why we are saying this is because we understand that the past will always filter through to the now but what we are saying is to **not make the past the future. To acknowledge the pains that you have had in your life but allow the pain to propel you forward, So that you are blossoming as a beautiful self.**

From your past you can educate yourself and others and say:

"I have been through experiences in the past. I will now take those energies that I have been through, the positive and negative experiences to move me on and into the future and in 'The Now'. I have learned from these experiences as they propel me to create positivity in my future".

We, the Kemetians, are saying to you that life is about learning, but the opportunities to learn presents themselves when you are quiet, when your mind is quiet, your soul is quiet and you are spirituality quiet. In this quiet moment you can connect with yourself, all your thoughts, all your ideas and your heart beat: listen to it as you connect. Whilst you are doing this, take a deep breath.

So in this revelation today we are calling for the power of you. The power of your gifts inside of you to blossom and this is what we are calling self-empowerment. We are calling for you to connect inside, **to follow your gut instinct and to hear the voice inside your head and heart advancing you on and propelling you forward**. This practice will assist you in this time. This will assist you to advise other people and for you to find your own path.

Self-empowerment is for you and nobody else can tell you what to do or how to do it. To give you that power to know, to instinctively feel what's inside of you is right.

Do not make yourself wrong -you will know inside of you what is right; what action you may take that is right and what action that you may take that is wrong. You are inbuilt with that facility and if you feel that you are having doubts sit down with yourself and then breathe in and out.

You see in ancient Kemet or ancient Egypt, we had to feel confident and empowered. You can see our actions have left a legacy on the whole universe. People visit Kemet and feel the vibrations of our monuments and these vibrations have affected the Universe.

We were proud of ourselves, we felt comfortable with ourselves and nobody could tell us otherwise. We did have negatives and there were many, many, many fights, arguments but whoever the next pharaoh was, he/she would feel that sense of pride and they would then illustrate this pride in all of their work. The monuments and statues and pyramids show that we were very proud and very honored. We were here on planet earth to complete our mission and we were happy with ourselves. We observe the inner contentment and inner peace that many people in this time are not experiencing. We are saying that many people may find it helpful to breathe more than they are doing normally. To take in big breathes, breathe out and full your stomach up with air. Let those negative thoughts drip away one by one. Allowing you to feel safe in your own skin ; allowing all the words of what other people say to leave you.

You see why we have come to speak to you today, is because we were very comfortable in ourselves. We understood about all of the outside external influences. They did not affect us because of the time we lived in and in our time we could be more focused and connected with the external natural world; the trees, the birds, the moon and the sun. We were concerned with the naturalness of life. So we are calling for you to recognize that once your self -esteem is raised you will be self- empowered. To raise your self-esteem is to sit quietly and to eradicate all of the negative words that bombard you daily. The negative words that say you are not good enough. You can't do something, you are not attractive enough, you are not slim enough they all start with NOTS. Take the word NOT out and replace into your psyche words such as:

I am attractive.
I am beautiful.
I am clever.
My soul is filled with light.
My spirit is energised with golden light.
I can hear words of the spirit of the universal force.
I am a part of the God force and whatever I look like physically is not important.
What is important is what I am contented inside.

With those words your energy levels should rise and you should have a spark of light. Realise that you are here to give what you can and to walk on the road to your path in this time. Be contented with your physical self! Many people want to change things about themselves and that is fine as long as you are not changing to fit in with somebody else's ideas of what beauty may be. You may speak positively to yourselves on a daily basis To raise your self-esteem you may say: **"I am beautiful inside and outside"** You may not believe it but keep saying these words daily, every other day, every other week, the words will help you to raise your vibration. When you say beauty, it is of the Mind Body and Spirit. It is not just the physical beauty, it is a deep beauty and from your beautiful essence you will speak words of positivity. There will be days when you feel negative but you will say your mantra:

I am beautiful inside and outside. My self-esteem is raised with this acknowledgement. I will let nobody else tell me what to say or how I shall look. What I shall say is that I am connected with the Divine source of who I am.

By The Kemetian collective

Chapter 19 Exercise:
Positive self-esteem

☥ This chapter is about reformatting your mind to create positive self-esteem and empowerment.

☥ Read this chapter on the Kemetians. Consider how they thought and lived their lives. What have you learnt from them?

☥ Use the daily mantras for a month and then monitor how you feel.

☥ Say kind words to yourself and repeat:

☥ I:
Accept myself
Forgive myself
Open my heart to my self

☥ I:
Practice self-love and nurturing.
Most importantly say:

☥ "I walk with my head held high with power. I Love myself"

☥ Consider ways in which you can help others to heal with the above affirmations.

Chapter 20
HOW THE EGO CAN STOP ABUNDANCE

We, the Spirits the Guardians of planet Earth, come to you on this Earth day. We are looking at the global experience. We, the Guardians of planet Earth, are a spiritual collective who have come forth today to explain to you the EGO. It is the wise man, the indigenous man, that connects with nature and who they really are as people. Many of you whom have come forth today in this planet are losing the important connection with nature. Nature teaches you, in this present time, that you are a spirit and a soul. Nature defines that you are an element of the Divine expression. The Creator's expression and the Creator's expressions have to behave in a creator way filled with the powers of the Creator.

Your lesson in this time is to walk the road of life and this journey is one of stumbling blocks. These stumbling blocks are for you to overcome, so that you can manifest as a Divine person. The ego can certainly manifest, but it is there in part, to create your personality not for you to allow it to be a person in its own right. When it becomes a person in its own right, then it is in control of you and you are not in control of it. When you start to behave in such a way that the ego is in control, the ego then uses your feelings, emotions and mind, bringing them all together to rule making an example of other individuals in a negative way.
The ego is in charge when you feel yourself going into a negative paradigm and saying negative word vibrations or when you are feeling negative thoughts and creating judgments. When you make people wrong, then you know that the ego is in charge. The ego energy is oscillating on planet Earth, in a micro and macro level.

Now, what we are saying is the ego uses the mind, word, actions, patterns and sound in a negative way. When you allow yourself to run with this energy of emotions and feelings, what is created then is the negative vibration of the ego. This energy becomes a volcano of words, sounds and body language of which, in turn, hits another person. You see this vibration in politicians; they have the biggest egos. They want to draw your energy and use it for their own power. The ego is an energy manufacturer and when the ego has your energy it is like a powerhouse. It takes your energy and it becomes bigger and bigger. Those of you born on planet Earth have to be careful of this, as the energy needs material objects to make it bigger and bigger. When it is not material objects, it is other people's mind-sets and their mental energy.

It is an energy vortex and is energy taking. The energy takers, such as the pastors, the men in cloth, the people in 'high' positions on planet Earth allow themselves to be in control to take your energy, to control and manipulate the whole entire Earth, bringing the Earth in a dense vibration with nothing going forward in the light. The ego is running away from the light. Thus the energy of the ego will bring to it a musical vibration, that is not positive and word vibrations from others who are not positive. This will go on to create and manifest more of this negativity and this is where you are on this planet.

We, the Guardians of the planet Earth, have watched this go on and we now see that this is getting worse -especially within individual interactions. We have come forth and we are asking you Neferatiti, to write about this concern of ours, in your book.

What we are saying to each and every individual is to be mindful of your utterances, your energy and the collective responsibility to each other on this planet Earth. Be gentle in your words and deeds. Check out where your ideas are coming from. Where are you coming from with your communication? How can your words and actions help or hinder the other person? Do not allow your communication to foster feelings and emotions into the negative. Be mindful of the energy that you are vibrating.

GOING FORWARD

Imagine if all of you raised your vibration.

Beginning and ending each day in a positive alignment. Bringing positive energies and thoughts with you. Imagine if all of you cleared your mind, meditated and listened to positive music. If the humans did these things, the vibration on planet Earth would begin to change from its current dense place. Now planet Earth has to come into alignment, as you know, with the other planets and the other universes. Planet Earth is not in alignment and has a long way to go and not much time.

The individuals on this planet, although they say that they are positive, their actions are not of positivity. Their word and sound vibrations are not positive and we can hear it in the ethereal world.

We have called for healing on this planet but the individuals on this planet have forgotten about healing. **If each individual removes their mind from the negative mind-set and allow the mind to rest and the body to rest and the soul and the spirit to rest, then the vibration will come to a period where its vibrations will be lifted. It will then slowly come into alignment with the other planets.**

Currently the planet Earth is on a road to a collision. This road is not the best route for planet Earth. So the message today is for individuals who now have forgotten the indigenous communities, to try to remember and give back something to these communities that are in need of assistance, so they do not die. Allow their words and spirits to resonate by connecting with them and listening to their wisdom.

GOING FORWARD

Individuals:

Consider that when you give, you will receive. When you give out energy, you will get back energy. Good energy gets back good energy. Bad energy receives back bad energy. You spend your day giving to people from your heart, then the Earth, will give you back positive.

Each individual consider your daily interactions. How are you spending the day? We are not saying that you should be positive alone but we are saying to be mindful. To breathe in and to get off the negative, egoistic vibration through music, by meditation, by clearing, by swimming, by exercise, dancing and being physical. All of these things will help you to move off the vibration of non-positivity. Clear your ego by connecting other and going out to laugh. All of these things change the vibration and calls in the positive spirits into alignment of where you can be. Calling the positivity into your self. Each day ask for a clearing of the mind to allow your spirits, your angels, your guides or the Creator, whichever energy to help you in a positive way. Call in for bright colours bringing in clearance of your mind, body and soul. As you receive the positive clearance from the negativity, you go forth. So these are the lessons today. We are calling for the upliftment of this dense planet, the upliftment of each and every individual that runs around thinking that he or she has ultimate power. The Creator has the ultimate power. Everything is everything. You are everything and everything is you. So bring together the light in your life. Change the planets vibration by your thoughts, your words, the music and as we said, the oxygen. When you are having repetitive thoughts put on some music and stop the ego from going forth on its negative axis. Allow the ego to go forth on a positive axis.

Once the dynamic of the ego changes, it can open its heart. Ego can listen to music. Ego can help others. Ego can give love to others without expecting anything back but give anyway. Each of you has to do individual work to reach the state of nirvana. Each of you can transform your ego to become positive.

Raise yourself up and walk upright. Call the energies to clear you. We the guardians of the planet Earth, say this is not an Extra-terrestrial venture, we are coming from the heart wanting to stop the volcanoes, the floods and earthquakes and the planet going down.

Mantra for healing the environment:

We are calling for the whole healing of this environment, every space and every corner. The waters, the seas. We are calling for a healing of the souls in these places. When the physical individuals on planet Earth heal, the souls heal, the departed ones heal because they are in need of the positive energy too.

Without a rising of these energies, there will be more deaths and passing over of individuals into the ethereal world. We are holding the energy of those that are alive and those that have passed. We are holding the continuum of energy.

We can see clearly and we want to ask you all to think of peace and love and light. Think of ways to create peace, love and light in every situation. Not only for yourselves but for others.

Before we go, look at the indigenous people on this planet and see what you can learn from them and their spirituality and their respect for their environment.

Go forth each and every one of you. Peace love and vibration in your thoughts and your sounds.

Amen Ra Guardians of planet
(A group of spirits that are here to guard and protect planet Earth in this time).

Chapter 20 Exercise:
The ego

☥ *The idea of the ego is very hard to detect in yourself but once you identify that you are acting from an egotist standpoint. You can then remove the negative ego and relate to others from your heart.*

☥ *EXPERIMENT WITH RELATING TO OTHERS BY SPEAKING FROM YOUR HEART*

☥ *For the following week observe your actions and words. When are you relating from an ego standpoint?*

☥ *Write the incidents down.*

☥ *What can you do to change this and transform your communication to one that is from your heart?*

☥ *Discuss the results with a close friend.*

Chapter 21
OUTRO

Greetings readers, I am glad you have been welcomed into the world of connecting with spiritual beings. I have decided to leave this last lament for the outro. It's something you can take forward to change the vibration of Mother Earth.

Meditation and vibration is spoken about in depth in this book and it is essential to all spiritual and psychic work leading to transformation of the self and others. In order to connect with beings of light and positive energy, your mind will need to be open to this energy. In the moments that you are connecting, you will need to be able to hear and believe the words that come through from the spiritual into the physical world. Many people have asked, 'how do I meditate?' and 'how do I to connect with my ancestors and my God?'

This book is an answer to their desire. There are many transformation books on the market but as far as I know none of them have been able to tap into the spiritual world for guidance on this topic. I have decided to change that trend. The spiritual world, my guides, ancestors and the universal energy that I call GOD (male and female energy) has written this book to which I have been a channel. If you have chosen to read this book, it must mean that you are open-minded to the spiritual world. What I ask of you when reading this book, is to please be open-minded to the message and feel the vibration of what is being said. The message is the most important essence for me. Each message has come from the spirit world in order to change and improve the physical world. I have included my personal experiences; these have been learning experiences of which I felt I needed to share. Which in turn, may help others.

We are all bombarded by negativity all day and every day. The light of positivity is blinded and now the spiritual world is calling for some balance on planet Earth. The negative vibrations are affecting all elements of the earth causing it to erupt and become destabilised.

Whilst reading the words of this book, consider what you can do to change things, by raising the vibration and creating a balance in this time.

This book talks to all races and religions, as now is time to move the planet onto another vibratory level. To do this, start with the mind and believing that you can do so. When your mind is in a good place the rest of your body i.e. soul, spirit and physical body can follow. Everyone on this planet is already familiar with spirits, through the belief of ghosts, believing in God etc. So what I call for is for earth beings to open up their minds so that it is not only the, 'special people', i.e. the priests and the psychic ones that can speak to the spiritual world.

We all can do this. We all have the facility and we all have it within us but it starts with belief and calming down of the mind. This book considers the mind, body, soul and spirit and the transformation of those elements, creating a being that can oscillate at a high vibratory level. I ask you to consider who you are, and your vibration. Question how you can save this planet as I have considered these things. I am by all means not perfect but I do believe that the spiritual world has a lot to offer and this belief has led me to write this book with passion.

Chapter 22
THE GIFT TO HOLD IN YOUR HEART

I was inspired to write about Love after my partner kept badgering me to listen to a record that he was going to add to his up and coming film. I knew the song but never really listened or took deep notice of it. There are so many songs that you hear but not many come from a deep place and this song's vibration for me was very special. The song is called, Everything Must Change written by Benard Ighner. After several discussions about this song, I decided to actually listen to it. Many artists have sang it, with great power and enthusiasm.

The lyrics and the power of the person who sang it inspired me to write. The energy of this song touched deep within for me. It came with a strong message that it is time for the inhabitants on planet earth to change.

Change to a vibration of healing and positivity. The writing of this book really comes from my heart with a message to change this planet before we totally self-destruct.

I have noticed that from the 1980s, the focus has been on materialism and individuality. This focus of the, **ME** mentality has gone on for several years but what has it brought? I feel that it has brought the focus away from the heart to the thinking mind and intelligence. All of this is good, but we need some balance. If you have read this book you may begin to realise that it comes from a deep place and this deep place is Love. Let's now start the change, a movement to call for the FORGIVENESS for the wrongs that others have done, moving on in Love.

We need more Love, more kindness and more respect for each other. This can only come with Change. Change from deep within. The mind, spirit, body and soul change.

When we decide to embark on this change (and it is dependent on our individual experiences of change) we will see a more nurturing environment. An environment that our grand children will live in happily and in peace. Leaving fear and worry behind.

This change starts with each of us taking the responsibility of our words, actions and deeds to others, the animal kingdom, Mother Earth, our environment and the planet that we live on.

Let the loving peaceful and nurturing movement start with you, today and let's start NOW!

Everything must change, nothing stays the same
Everyone must change, no one stays the same
The young become the old and mysteries do unfold
'Cause that's the way of time, nothing and no one goes unchanged
There are not many things in life you can be sure of
Except rain comes from the clouds, sun lights up the sky
And humming birds do fly, winter turns to spring
A wounded heart will heal but never much too soon

Benard Ighner

About the author

Neferatiti Ife holds a Post graduate Diploma in Therapeutic Counselling., Bachelors of Social Science degree in Social work and a Sociology Degree. Over the last 9 years she has developed her psychic channelling abilities, connecting with Ancient ancestral beings as well as Light beings from the ethereal world. These communications led to the publication of her first book, 'Conversations with the Blackman's God'. In addition Neferatiti has produced a range of channelled meditation CD's. Recently she has produced her own unique Transformation 44 deck Cards. These cards extends her unique approach to spirituality and wellbeing. The spiritual guidance, communication with Ancient ancestral beings, other light beings and Mother/Father Creator, has assisted Neferatiti to create further empowerment tools for individuals.

She now offers holistic healing workshops using both her cards and meditation modules to assist in the healing of physical and psychological dis-ease, past baggage and releasing inner potential. Neferatiti is emerging as one of the important new voices in expanding the understanding of the spirit world and connecting this knowledge for the transformation of individuals and the betterment of this planet.

Lightning Source UK Ltd.
Milton Keynes UK
UKHW020231260919
350442UK00008B/54/P